OWN IT! 1

A2 Key test content in *Own It!* Level 1 has been checked by Cambridge Assessment English for accuracy and level.

STUDENT'S BOOK
WITH PRACTICE EXTRA

Claire Thacker
with Melissa Wilson and Daniel Vincent

CAMBRIDGE UNIVERSITY PRESS

CONTENTS

STARTER

WELCOME!

VOCABULARY

Months

S.01 **1 Put the months in the correct order. Listen, check and repeat.**

April	☐	January	1	May	☐
August	☐	June	☐	November	☐
December	☐	July	☐	October	☐
February	☐	March	☐	September	☐

Get it right!

In English, months and days of the week start with a capital letter. Is it the same in your language?

2 Complete the sentences. Compare with a partner.

1 This month is ________ .
2 My birthday is in ________ .

Cardinal and ordinal numbers

3 Write the numbers.

1 The number of letters in my name. ______
2 The date today. ______
3 The number of people in my house. ______

LEARN TO LEARN

Learning numbers together

Learn and practise cardinal and ordinal numbers together.

23 twenty-three, 23rd twenty-third

S.02 **4 Listen. Circle the numbers you hear.**

1	a 17	b 70	3	a 12th	b 20th
2	a 13	b 30	4	a 51st	b 61st

Use it!

5 Take turns to say a cardinal number. Your partner says the ordinal number.

S.03 **6 Listen and complete the sentences with the date.**

1 Laura's birthday is on 24th July .
2 Onur's birthday is on ________ .
3 Bella's birthday is on ________ .
4 Nico's birthday is on ________ .

7 Complete the sentences. Tell your partner.

1 My birthday is on ________ .
2 Today is ________ .

Colours

S.04 **8 Add the colours and write the new colour. Listen, check and repeat.**

Purple ______ ______ ______

S.05 **9 Do the quiz with a partner. Circle the correct answer. Listen and check.**

THE GREAT BIG NUMBER QUIZ!!

1 The number of countries in the world is … .
a 195 b 100 c 95

2 … million people speak English as their first language.
a 3 b 36 c 360

3 There are … seconds in a year.
a 36,536,000 b 31,536,000 c 35,636,000

4 … million people have the same birthday as you.
a 19 b 6 c 10

READING
An online profile

1 **Look at the photos. Where do you think Diana and Thiago are from? Read the profiles quickly and check your answers.**

S.06 **2** **Read the profiles again. Are the sentences *T* (true) or *F* (false)?**

1. Diana is from Granada. T
2. Miranda is Turkish. ___
3. Diana's favourite place is her bedroom. ___
4. Thiago is from São Paulo. ___
5. Thiago's favourite colour is blue. ___
6. Thiago is good at football. ___

3 **Find nationalities in the profiles to match the countries.**

1. Spain Spanish
2. Mexico ___
3. Turkey ___
4. Brazil ___
5. the USA ___

4 **Complete the table with the countries and nationalities.**

Flag	Country	Nationality
	Australia	1 Australian
	2 ___	Canadian
	China	3 ___
	4 ___	German
	Poland	5 ___
	the UK	6 ___

Voice it!

5 **Complete the sentences with your ideas. Compare with a partner.**

1. Diana's bedroom is ___ because ___ .
2. Thiago's favourite colours are yellow and green because ___ .

Welcome to my life!

Home | Profile | Photos | Events

Hi! My name's Diana.
I'm from Granada in Spain.
I'm 13 years old.

In this photo, I'm with Miranda and Suki. They're my best friends. They aren't Spanish. Miranda's Mexican and Suki's Turkish.

My birthday is on 9th March. When is your birthday?

My favourite colour is blue.

My favourite place is my bedroom. Guess what colour it is!

My dream is to be a singer like Rihanna. She's brilliant! 🙂 Are you a good singer?

What's your name? How old are you? Let me know! 🙂

Home | Profile | Photos | Events

Hello! My name's Thiago. I'm from Brasília. It's the capital of Brazil. I'm Brazilian. I'm 14. I'm with Bruno and Victor in this photo. They're my best friends. We're at the same American school, but I'm not in their class.

My favourite colours are yellow and green. Can you guess why?

My favourite number is 10.

My dream is to be a footballer like Neymar Júnior. He's amazing! I'm good, too! 🙂 Are you a football fan?

What's your name? Where are you from? Write soon!

LANGUAGE IN ACTION

Subject pronouns and possessive adjectives

Watch video S.1
Where is Isabella from?
What is Martine's dream?

Subject pronouns	Possessive adjectives	Subject pronouns	Possessive adjectives
I	[1] ______	it	**its**
you	[2] ______	we	**our**
he	**his**	they	**their**
she	**her**		

1 **Complete the examples in the table above. Use the profiles on page 5 to help you.**

2 **Circle the correct words.**

1 Alana is (my) / I best friend.
2 *Our* / *We* aren't from Brazil. *Our* / *We* 're from Spain.
3 *Her* / *She* name is Luna. *Her* / *She* 's 13.
4 *Their* / *They* names are Kit and Bella. *Their* / *They* aren't British.

Verb *be*

Affirmative	I[1]'m (**am**) from Granada. She[2]___ (**is**) brilliant! He[3]___ (**is**) amazing! We[4]___ (**are**) at the same American school. They[5]___ (**are**) my best friends.
Negative	They [6]______ Spanish. Miranda **isn't** Turkish. I[7]______ in their class.
Questions and short answers	How old [8]________ you? [9]________ you a football fan? Yes, I **am**. / No, I**'m not**. **Is** Thiago 12? Yes, he **is**. / No, he **isn't**. **Are** Bruno and Victor Brazilian? Yes, they **are**. / No, they **aren't**.

3 **Complete the examples in the table above. Use the profiles on page 5 to help you.**

S.07 **4** **Complete the profile with the correct form of *be*. Guess the person. Listen and check.**

His birthday [1] __is__ (✓) on 1st March.
He [2]________ (✗) American.
He [3]________ (✓) Canadian. My favourite songs [4]________ (✓) *Boyfriend* and *Sorry*.
[5]________ (?) he your favourite singer?
____

5 **Write questions with the verb *be*.**

1 you / 12? Are you 12?
2 you / from / Ankara? ______________
3 your best friends / in your class?
____
4 your teacher / English?
____
5 today / 19th June? ______________

Use it!

6 **Ask and answer the questions in Exercise 5.**

Question words

7 **Match the question words with their functions.**

1 What — d
2 Where
3 When
4 How old
5 Who

a age
b people
c places
d things
e time and dates

8 **Complete the questions with *is* or *are*.**

1 Where __are__ you from?
2 How old ________ you?
3 When ________ your birthday?
4 Who ________ your best friend?
5 What ________ your favourite colour?

Use it!

9 **Ask and answer the questions in Exercise 8.**

VOCABULARY AND LISTENING

Classroom objects

S.08 **1 Match the words in the box with the objects in the picture 1–12. Listen, check and repeat.**

board	1	calculator	☐	chair	☐	dictionary	☐
door	☐	notebook	☐	pen	☐	pencil	☐
poster	☐	ruler	☐	table	☐	window	☐

LEARN TO LEARN

Recording vocabulary

Divide the pages in your notebook to record new vocabulary. Write a translation and draw a picture to help you remember the words.

Classroom objects	Translation	Picture

2 **Organise your notebook and write new vocabulary from this unit.**

3 **Test a partner. Say a word in your language. Your partner says it in English. Can you remember all the new words?**

A talk

S.09 **4 Listen and circle the correct answer.**

Stefan is …

a a teacher. b a student.

S.09 **5 Listen again. Circle the correct answer.**

1 Stefan is in Year *7* / *10*.
2 Stefan *is* / *isn't* a friendly person.
3 It's the students' *first* / *second* day at the school.
4 At the end, Luiza *is* / *isn't* in the classroom.

Use it!

6 Answer the questions with a partner.

1 What classroom objects are on your table?
2 What is in your bag?

LANGUAGE IN ACTION

whose + possessive pronouns

Watch video S.2
What colour is Mia's pen?
What classroom objects are there?

Whose ... ?	Possessive pronouns
Whose dictionary is this?	It's **mine**.
	It's **yours**.
	It's **his**.
	It's **hers**.
	It's **ours**.
	It's **theirs**.

this, that, these, those	
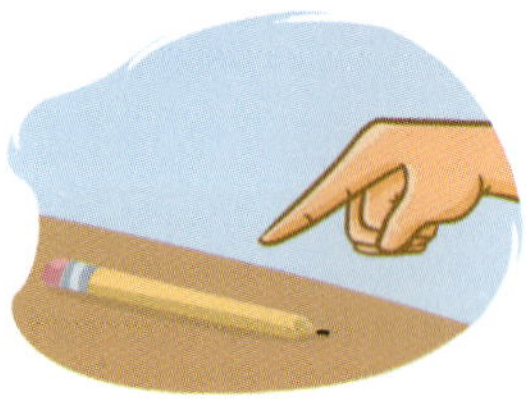 **This** is my pencil.	 **That** is my calculator.
 **These** are my notebooks.	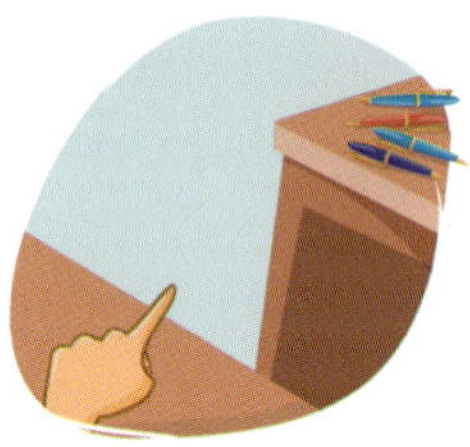 **Those** are my pens.

1 **Look at the table above. Complete the second sentence with a possessive pronoun.**

1 It's your pencil. It's _yours_.
2 That's his notebook. That's ________.
3 This table is my table. This table is ________.
4 Those are our chairs. Those are ________.
5 Is this your calculator? Is this ________?
6 Are these her pens? Are these ________?

S.10 **2** **Write the questions. Listen and match the questions with the answers.**

1 book / whose / this / is
   Whose book is this? [b]
2 posters / those / are / whose
   ________ [ ]
3 are / pens / whose / these
   ________ [ ]
4 that / ruler / whose / is
   ________ [ ]

a It's his.
b It's mine.
c They're hers.
d They're ours.

Imperatives

Close the door! [ ]	Don't be late! [ ]

3 **Look at the table above. Which sentence is positive (✓)?**

S.11 **4** **Complete the instructions with the verbs in the box. Listen and check.**

don't forget ~~don't write~~ listen to use write

1 _Don't write_ on the desks!
2 ________ new words in your notebook!
3 ________ to bring your pen!
4 ________ your teacher!
5 ________ a dictionary!

S.12 **5** **Listen and follow the instructions.**

Use it!

6 **Take turns to give your partner instructions. Use classroom objects or your own ideas.**

Pick up your pen!

Write your birthday!

WRITING
An informal letter

1 Read Gloria's letter. Who is Mrs Weston?

29 Upper Road
Wilmslow
Cheshire
SK52 0TY

16th September

Dear Mrs Weston,

1 [ ] My name is Gloria Rodriguez **and** I'm 13. I'm from Ottowa in Canada. I'm Canadian.

2 [ ] I'm a student at the International School. It's my first day in this school. I'm happy! I'm in class 7A. That's your class!

3 [ ] The students here are from all over the world. My best friends are Marco **and** Leona. They're in my class. They aren't Canadian like me. Marco is Italian **and** Leona is German.

4 [ ] My favourite colour is pink **and** my favourite place is my English classroom. My dream is to be a teacher – just like you!

Best wishes,

Gloria

2 Match topics a–d with paragraphs 1–4.

a Information about your favourite things
b Information about you
c Information about your friends
d Information about your school

3 Read Gloria's letter again. Which information isn't in the letter? ______

name age birthday country
nationality names of her best friends
favourite colour and place dream

4 Look at the *Useful language* box and complete the information with words from Gloria's letter.

Useful language

to start: [1] ______ + *Mr* (man) or *Mrs/Miss* (woman) + person's surname,
to end: *All the best,* or [2] ______
to join two ideas in one sentence: [3] ______

5 Join the sentences with *and*.

1 My name is Hugo. I'm 13 years old.
______
2 I'm Japanese. I'm from Tokyo.
______
3 My favourite number is 15. My favourite colour is red.
______

Write an informal letter.

PLAN

6 Decide what information to include in each paragraph. Use the information in Exercise 2 to help you.

WRITE

7 Write your letter. Remember to include four paragraphs, the address and date, and expressions from the *Useful language* box.

CHECK

8 Do you …

- introduce yourself and give your name, age and nationality?
- use *and* to join ideas?
- say what your dream is?

1 FRIENDS AND FAMILY

LEARNING OUTCOMES

I can …

- understand texts about families and a festival
- phone a friend
- write an email
- understand how to use *have got*; possessive *'s*; questions with *How many …?*
- talk about families and describe people
- draw pictures to remember words and increase my vocabulary.

Start it!

1 Look at the photo. How are families different?
2 Before you watch, are friends family?
3 Where are Laura and Andrés from? Watch and check.
4 Which is your favourite family? Why?

Watch video 1.1

p13

Language in action 1.2

p15

Language in action 1.3

p16

Everyday English 1.4

p18

Globetrotters 1.5

VOCABULARY

Family members

1 (1.01) **Look at Beth's family tree. Match nine words in the box with the people a–i. Listen and check.**

aunt	☐	brother	☐	cousin	☐
dad	☐	daughter	☐	grandad	a
granddaughter	☐	grandma	☐	grandson	☐
husband	☐	mum	☐	nephew	☐
niece	☐	sister	☐	son	☐
uncle	☐	wife	☐		

2 (1.02) **Look again at Beth's family tree. Complete the answers with words from Exercise 1. Listen, check and repeat.**

1 Andy + Sara = husband and _wife_
2 Lizzie + Olga = mum and ______
3 Amanda + Theo = grandma and ______
4 Ryan + Beth = ______ and ______
5 Lizzie + Theo = ______ and ______
6 Theo + Beth = ______ and ______

3 Complete the lists with the family words in Exercise 1.

Male: _brother_ ______ ______ ______
______ ______ ______ ______

Female: ______ ______ ______ ______
______ ______ ______ ______

Both male and female: ______

LEARN TO LEARN

Making connections (1)

Think of examples from your own life to help you remember new words.

4 Draw your family tree. Use Beth's family tree to help you.

5 Don't show your family tree. Take turns to say the name of a person in your family. Can your partner guess who they are?

Carlos. *Is he your brother?* *No, he isn't. Try again.*

Use it!

6 Imagine you are a famous person. Write sentences to describe your family. Tell your partner. Can they guess who you are?

I'm British. My brother is Harry. My wife is Kate. My children are George, Charlotte and Louis.

Are you Prince William? *Yes, I am.*

Explore it!

Guess the correct answer.

A Canadian woman, Vera Sommerfeld, is a great-great-great grandma. There are … generations of women in her family.

a two b four c six

Find an interesting family fact. Write a question for your partner to answer.

READING
A webpage

1 **Tell your partner two things you know about the circus and two things you want to know about the topic.**

1.03 **2** **Read the webpage. What is it about?**

1 A visit to the circus
2 Life in a circus family
3 A circus school

MEET THE *Flying* CORTES FAMILY

Ysabella Wallenda-Cortes isn't from a typical family. She's from a circus family. Ysabella is a trapeze artist like her parents. Her parents' names are Robinson and Alida. She's got two brothers, Lucas and Tomas, but she hasn't got any sisters.

Ysabella's uncle and aunt are in the circus, too. Her uncle Alex is her dad's brother and he's an acrobat and a trapeze artist. Her aunt Aurelia is her mum's sister and she's one of Ysabella's teachers. Her grandparents, Olinka and Tino, are also part of the circus. Olinka isn't a performer any more. Her job is to help the rest of the family. Tino is in his 60s but he's still a tightrope walker. Lucas and Tomas haven't got jobs in the circus … yet!

Where is home? They've got two homes – one in the USA and a mobile home. The mobile home is also a school during tours. Imagine a school on wheels!

3 **Find words in the webpage to match the photos.**

4 **Read the webpage again. Complete the sentences with the correct family words.**

Ysabella's …

1 parents are trapeze artists.
2 ________ is an acrobat and a trapeze artist.
3 ________ is a circus teacher.
4 ________ aren't circus performers yet.

5 **Correct the sentences.**

1 Ysabella Cortes is a tightrope walker.
Ysabella Cortes isn't a tightrope walker.
She's a trapeze artist.
2 Robinson and Alida are brother and sister.
3 Lucas and Tomas are cousins.
4 Alida and Aurelia are friends.

Voice it!

6 **Discuss the questions.**

1 What do you think is a typical family?
2 Is family life in the circus like your family life? Why / Why not?
3 What are the good and bad things about life in the circus?

Finished? p118 Ex 1

Watch video 1.2
True or false?
Tess has got two brothers.
Marco has got a big family.

LANGUAGE IN ACTION

have got: affirmative and negative

I/you/we/they	*he/she/it*
They **have** (**'ve**) **got** two homes.	Ysabella **has** [1](*'s*) *got* two brothers.
Lucas and Tomas **have not** [2](________) ________ jobs in the circus.	She **has not** [3](________) ________ any sisters.

1 Complete the examples in the table above. Use the webpage on page 12 to help you.

2 Circle the correct form of *have got*. Check your answers in the webpage on page 12.

1. Robinson *has got* / *hasn't got* a sister in the circus.
2. Alida *has got* / *hasn't got* a sister in the circus.
3. Olinka and Tino *have got* / *haven't got* any grandsons in the circus.
4. Ysabella *has got* / *hasn't got* an aunt and an uncle in the circus.

1.04 **3** Complete the text with the correct form of *have got*. Listen and check.

Meet this week's circus stars …

Bibi and Bichu Tesfamariam are brothers and they're from Ethiopia. They [1] *haven't got* (–) any sisters. Ethiopia [2]________ (–) a circus tradition but Bibi and Bichu are brilliant jugglers. They [3]________ (+) a circus school in Ethiopia. It [4]________ (+) 150 students. They [5]________ (+) their own circus too, called Circus Abyssinia, with some amazing Ethiopian acrobats. We think Bibi and Bichu [6]________ (+) a great future!

Possessive *'s*

Alex is her dad**'s** brother.	Her parents**'** names are Robinson and Alida.

4 Look at the table above. Complete the sentences. Use the words in brackets with *'s* or *s'*.

1. *Aurelia's* niece is Ysabella. (Aurelia)
2. Alida is ________ wife. (Robinson)
3. ________ names are Ysabella, Alex, Robinson and Alida. (the trapeze artists)
4. ________ grandparents are Olinka and Tino. (Ysabella)
5. Aurelia is ________ sister. (Alida)

Use it!

5 Write true and false sentences with *'s* or *s'* and *have got*. Use the ideas below or your own ideas.

My ________'s name ________.
________ got ________.
My ________s' house ________.
________ got ________.
My sister's classroom ________ got ________.
I haven't got ________.
My grandparents' house is pink. They've got a big garden.

6 Take turns to say your sentences. Can your partner guess the false sentences?

My mum's name is Sandra. She's got two sisters.

False! Your mum's name is Emma.

Finished? p118 Ex 2

VOCABULARY AND LISTENING

Describing people

1.05 **1** **Complete the table with the words for describing people in the box. Listen, check and repeat.**

beard	blonde	brown (x2)	freckles
glasses	grey (x2)	long	moustache
red	short (x2)	tall	wavy

Eyes	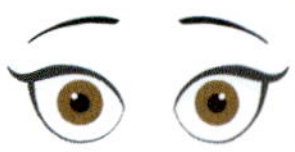	brown ______ ______
Hair style		______ ______ ______
Hair colour		______ ______ ______ ______
Height		______ ______
Other features		______ ______ ______ ______

LEARN TO LEARN

Drawing pictures

Drawing pictures can help you to remember new words.

2 **Draw pictures of the words in Exercise 1.**

Describing people

brown eyes 

3 **Cover the words and show your pictures to a partner. Can they guess the correct words?**

Get it right!

Adjectives go before nouns in English.

brown eyes **NOT** ~~eyes brown~~

Use it!

4 **Describe the people. Use words from Exercise 1.**

5 **Work in pairs. Take turns to describe a member of your family. Can your partner guess who they are?**

He's tall. He's got short brown hair.

Is it your dad?

Yes, it is. / No, it isn't.

A conversation

1.06 **6** **Look at the photo and listen. Who is the actor?**

1.06 **7** **Listen again. Circle the correct answers.**

The actor …

1. is *American* / *Australian*.
2. has got *blue* / *brown* eyes.
3. has got two *brothers* / *sisters*.
4. has got *an Australian* / *a Spanish* wife.
5. has got *two daughters and a son* / *two sons and a daughter*.

Watch video 1.3
Has she got blue eyes?
How many brothers has she got?

LANGUAGE IN ACTION

have got questions

Have they **got** any children?	**Has** he **got** blue eyes?	How many brothers and sisters [1] *has* he *got*?
Yes, they **have**.	Yes, he [2] ______.	He**'s got** two brothers.
No, they [3] ______.	No, he **hasn't**.	He [4] ______ ______ any sisters.

Pronunciation p141

1 Complete the examples in the table above.

2 (1.10) Write the questions and answers about the famous people in the quiz below. Circle the correct answer. Listen and check.

THIS WEEK'S *star* INTERVIEW

We've got the questions.
Have you got the answers?

1 How many / brothers and sisters / Daniel Radcliffe?

How many brothers and sisters has Daniel Radcliffe got?

a one brother

He's got one brother.

b (✗) brothers or sisters

He hasn't got any brothers or sisters.

2 Scarlett Johansson / a brother?

______

a a twin brother

______

b (✗) a twin sister

______

3 Mila Kunis / green eyes?

______

a (✗) blue eyes

______

b (✗) one green eye and one brown eye

______

3 Work in pairs. Write three questions like the ones in Exercise 2 about famous people. Ask another pair. Can they guess the answer?

1 ______
2 ______
3 ______

Use it!

4 Write a class quiz. Write questions with the correct form of *have got*.

1 brown eyes
______
2 a twin brother or sister
______
3 a pet
______
4 a phone
______
5 a niece or nephew
______

5 Ask the people in your class your quiz questions. Write down their answers.

Have you got brown eyes?

Yes, I have.

No, I haven't. I've got grey eyes.

6 Compare your answers with your classmates. What is interesting or surprising?

Finished? p118 Ex 3

SPEAKING
Phoning a friend

1.11 **1 Listen to the conversation. Who is Jack?**

LILY [1] Hey , Evan.
EVAN Hi, Lily. Are you alright? [2] ________?
LILY OK, thanks. [3] ________________?
EVAN [4] ________, thanks. So, how's school?
LILY It's good.
EVAN Have you got any new friends?
LILY Yes, I have. I've got one new friend. His name's Jack.
EVAN Cool! I've got a new boy in my class. His name's Jack, too.
LILY Has he got wavy black hair and blue eyes?
EVAN Yes, he has. That's funny! Maybe it's the same boy. Imagine if it is!
LILY That's so not funny, Evan!
EVAN Got to go! [5] ________!
LILY OK. [6] ________________.

1.11 **2 Complete the conversation with the phrases from the *Useful language* box. Listen and check.**

Useful language

Bye! Hey, (Evan). Hi, (Lily). How are things?
OK/Fine, thanks. You? See you later.

3 Look at the *Everyday English* box. Find and underline the phrases in the conversation.

Watch video 1.4
Everyday English

Are you alright? Cool! Got to go!
That's funny! That's so not funny!

4 Work with a partner. Practise the conversation.

PLAN

5 Write questions to ask your friend on the phone. Use the ideas below.

School? ________________

____

New friends? ________________

____

Family? ________________

____

SPEAK

6 Practise the phone conversation with your partner. Remember to use *have got*, the vocabulary from this unit and expressions from the *Useful language* and *Everyday English* boxes.

CHECK

7 Work with another pair. Listen to their phone conversation and complete the notes.

School: ________________

New friends: ________________

Family: ________________

Your new school penfriend is Martin, from England. Write to him below.

Hello Martin,

1 ☐ I'm Javi and I'm from Montijo, a small town in the west of Spain. I've got a big house and a very big family!

2 ☐ I've got six brothers and one sister. My brother, Dani, is my twin. He's tall. He's got short straight brown hair and brown eyes, like me. He's my brother and my friend! My sister, Claudia, is ten. She's got long brown hair, blue eyes and lots of freckles! I've got a pet rabbit. His name's Thumper! My best friend's name is Toni. He's funny!

3 ☐ Here's a photo of me with Dani (he's got a red shirt) and Claudia. We're in my uncle's garden.

4 ☐ Have you got a big family? Have you got any pets? Who's your best friend?

Write soon!

Javi

WRITING
An informal email

1 Look at the photo. Which boy is Javi? Read his email and find the answer.

2 Match topics a–d with paragraphs 1–4.

a Javi's questions for Martin
b Family and friends
c Introduction and reason for writing
d Extra information

3 Read the email again and answer the questions.

1 How old is Javi's sister? ______
2 How many brothers and sisters has Javi got? ______
3 Who is Thumper? ______
4 Who is Javi's best friend? ______

4 Complete the *Useful language* box with examples from Javi's email.

Useful language

at the start: Hi, Hey, 1 ______

at the end: Email me soon, That's all for now, 2 ______ !

contractions: I'm, I've, 3 ______ , She's, 4 ______ , 5 ______ , Who's

symbols: use emojis to help express your feelings

Write an informal email to a new friend.

PLAN

5 Make notes about these things.

Age: ______
Family: ______
Pets: ______
Friend(s): ______

Decide what information to include in each paragraph. Use the information in Exercise 2 to help you.

WRITE

6 Write your email. Remember to include four paragraphs, the verbs *be* and *have got* and expressions from the *Useful language* box.

CHECK

7 Do you …

- use expressions to start and end your email?
- give information about you and your family in the second paragraph?
- ask questions in the last paragraph?

Finished? p118 Ex 4

AROUND THE WORLD

READING
An article

Globetrotters

Watch video 1.5
Children's Day

- What is Children's Day?
- When is Children's Day in Japan?
- Which city are the superheroes in?

1.12 **1** **Look at the photos. Where are the people? What is special about them? Read the article to check your answers.**

2 **Find words in the article that mean:**

1. two children born at the same time (n) ________
2. three children born at the same time (n) ________
3. four children born at the same time (n) ________
4. very young children (n) ________

3 **Read the article again. Circle the correct words.**

1. The Festival of Twins is one *week* / *day* long.
2. Pleucadeuc isn't a *big* / *small* town.
3. The festival is for twins, triplets and quadruplets from *France* / *all over the world.*
4. Geoffrey and Guillaume *have got some* / *haven't got any* photos as babies at the Festival of Twins.

Voice it!

4 **Discuss the questions.**

1. What is interesting about the Festival of Twins?
2. Have you got any twins in your family?
3. What do you think life is like as a twin?

Twins Day

France is the third biggest country in Europe and it's got a lot of different festivals. They've got a film festival in Cannes, music festivals in Paris and in Lyon, and there's a festival of lights!

But, perhaps one of the most unusual festivals of all is 'Deux et Plus' or 'Festival of Twins' on 15th August in the small town of Pleucadeuc in the northwest of France. More than 1,000 twins, triplets and quadruplets from all over the world meet in one place! Some look the same and some look different, some even speak their own language! Imagine that!

LEARN TO LEARN

Increasing your vocabulary

When you learn an adjective, it's a good idea to learn the opposite adjective. Learning word pairs increases your vocabulary.

5 **Write the opposite adjectives for words 1–4. Find and underline them in the article.**

1 big small_____ 3 normal _____
2 last _____ 4 old _____

6 **Close your books. Say an adjective from Exercise 5. Can your partner remember the opposite adjective?**

Explore it!

Guess the correct answer.

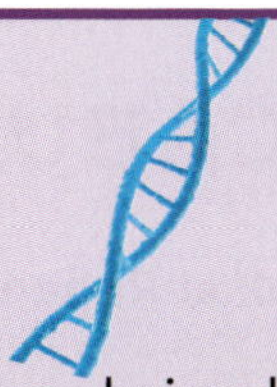

Identical twins have the same DNA, but they don't have the same …

a eye colour. b fingerprints. c hair colour.

Find two more interesting facts about twins. Choose your favourite fact and write a question for your partner to answer.

OWN IT! The Culture Project Teacher's Resource Bank

The festival has got its own traditions. Each twin, triplet, or quadruplet is usually in the same clothes with the same hairstyle! There are also a lot of interesting activities to do, like face painting, watching live music, dancing and playing fun games.

Geoffrey and Guillaume have got photos from their first visit to the festival of twins as babies. Now they are 13! 'It's a great day! We've got a lot of new friends this year.' Their new friends have all got the same DNA and one thing in common – they've all got brothers or sisters that look the same – or almost!!

1 REVIEW

VOCABULARY

1 **Look at Ruben's family tree. Complete the sentences.**

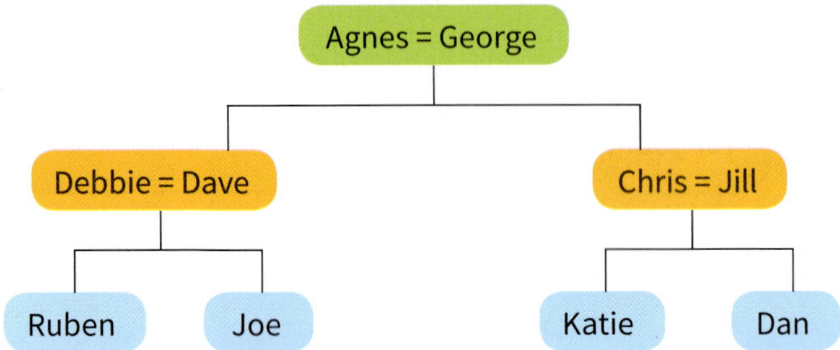

1 Joe: Agnes and George are my _______ .
2 Debbie and Dave: Ruben is our _______ .
3 Ruben: Katie and Dan are my _______ .
4 Jill: Ruben is my _______ .
5 Katie and Dan: Dave is our _______ .

2 **Complete the descriptions with words from the box.**

brown (x2) wavy glasses grey long red short (x2) tall

Kirsty is [1] _______ .
She's got [2] _______
_______ _______ hair.
She's got [3] _______ eyes.

Jack is [4] _______ .
He's got [5] _______
_______ hair.
He's got [6] _______ eyes.
He's got [7] _______ .

LANGUAGE IN ACTION

3 **Rewrite the sentences. Replace the underlined words with the words in brackets and *'s* or *s'*.**

1 Their names are Jack and Sara. (My parents)
____
2 Is that her phone? (Anna)
____
3 They're their bags. (my friends)
____
4 That's his bike. (Danny)
____

4 **Write the questions with *have got*. Answer them with the information in brackets.**

1 how many / sisters / you (four)
____
____
2 Toby / any cousins (✗)
____
____
3 you / a big family (✓)
____
____
4 your best friend / a pet (✓) (two cats)
____
____
5 you / a phone / in your bag (✗)
____
____

Self-assessment

I can use family words to talk about my family.
I can use adjectives to describe people.
I can use *have got* in affirmative and negative sentences.
I can use *have got* in questions.

LEARN TO ... ORGANISE YOUR NOTEBOOK

It's important to organise your notebook to help you to find your notes and study for exams.

1 Ask and answer with a partner.

1 Have you got a notebook?
2 Is it for all your subjects or for English only?
3 Are your notes easy or difficult to read?

2 Look at Omar's notebook. Match 1–4 with a–d.

1 Today's vocabulary c
2 Today's date ___
3 Today's homework ___
4 Today's grammar ___

a 23 September

b

have got	
I / you / we / they	have / haven't got ...
he / she / it	has / hasn't got ...

c

Family members	
dad husband brother son uncle nephew grandad grandson cousin	mum wife sister daughter aunt niece grandma granddaughter cousin

d Learn the family words from Unit 1.

3 Look at Azra's notebook. Is her notebook different from Omar's? How?

grammar / vocabulary / notes / homework

Verb *be*

Affirmative	Negative	Questions
I'm from Turkey.	I'm not from Turkey.	Am I Brazilian?
She's my sister.	She's isn't my sister.	Is she Mexican?
He's my brother.	He isn't my brother.	Is he from Ecuador?
We're at school.	We aren't at school.	Are we 12?
They're my cousins.	They aren't my cousins.	Are they at school?

4 Ask and answer with a partner.

1 What is good about Omar's notebook? What is good about Azra's?
2 What are some other ways to organise a notebook?
3 Which is your favourite way? Why?

OWN IT!

5 Discuss with a partner. Decide how to organise your notebook.

2 THAT'S LIFE!

LEARNING OUTCOMES

I can ...

- understand texts about daily routines
- ask and respond to interview questions
- write an article
- understand how to use the present simple and adverbs of frequency
- talk about daily routines and leisure activities
- identify word partners
- do a survey and present the results.

Start it!

1 Is the girl in the photo happy? Why / Why not?

2 Before you watch, what time is it in India now?

3 Which countries are in the video? Watch and check.

4 Which is your favourite activity in the video? Why?

Watch video 2.1

p25

Language in action 2.2

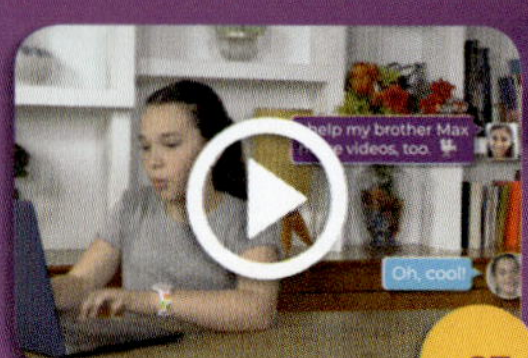

p27

Language in action 2.3

p28

Everyday English 2.4

VOCABULARY
Daily routines

1 *(2.01)* **Match eight of the activities in the box with the pictures a–h. Listen, check and repeat.**

brush your teeth	
check your phone	
do your homework	
get dressed	a
get up	
go home	
go to bed	
go to school	
have a shower	
have breakfast	
pack your bag	
wake up	

2 *(2.02)* **Which activities in the box in Exercise 1 are not in the pictures? Write them in the correct order. Listen, check and repeat.**

wake up

3 *(2.03)* **Listen to Eduardo talking about his day. Put all the activities in the correct order. Write 1–13 in the boxes in Exercise 1. Write two numbers in one box.**

LEARN TO LEARN

Word partners (1)

When you learn new words, think about the words that go with them. This will help you to remember them.

4 **Complete the table with activities from Exercise 1. Think of one more activity for each verb.**

go	*get*	*have*
to school		

Use it!

5 **Work in pairs. Take turns to say an activity from Exercise 1. Your partner guesses what time you do this activity.**

have breakfast *7 o'clock?* *No, try again.*

Explore it!

Guess the correct answer.

When you brush your teeth and leave the tap on, you use … litres of water every minute.

a two b five c ten

Find an interesting fact about another daily routine. Write a question for your partner to answer.

READING
A profile

A day in the life of ...

This is Amir from the Bajau tribe in Borneo. His life is unusual. He lives with his family in a house – but it's in the water. Amir doesn't know his age or the date of his birthday. The Bajau tribe don't count days and hours; they use the movement of the sea to count time.

Every morning, Amir wakes up early, but he doesn't have breakfast. He and his father go out in their boat. They swim in the water to look for food for the day. Amir and the people in his tribe can see really well under water. Amir catches a fish for breakfast and his father catches an octopus for dinner.

After breakfast, Amir usually meets his friends. They don't go to school and they don't study subjects like English. The older Bajau people teach them how to make nets and build boats.

In the afternoons, Amir and his friends dive into the water from bridges and they play in the water, too. It's their favourite place!

In the evenings, Amir's mother and sisters cook the octopus and then the family has dinner together. It's always delicious!

1 **Tell your partner three things you do after breakfast.**

2 **Read the profile. Say one surprising thing about Amir's routine.** (2.04)

3 **Find words in the profile to match the photos.**

a  ______

b  ______

c  ______

d  ______

4 **Read the profile again and complete the sentences.**

1 Amir lives in an unusual house with his family.
2 Amir and his father look for ______ every morning.
3 Amir can ______ really well under water.
4 Amir plays in the water in the ______.
5 Amir's favourite place is the ______.

5 **Are the sentences *T* (true) or *F* (false)?**

1 Amir's house isn't in the water. F
2 Amir's family has got a boat. ___
3 Before breakfast, Amir is in the water. ___
4 Amir isn't happy in water. ___
5 Amir hasn't got any sisters. ___

Voice it!

6 **Discuss the questions.**

1 How is Amir's life different from yours?
2 What do you like about Amir's day?

Finished? p119 Ex 1

Watch video 2.2
Name three things he does in the morning. Is he always on time for school?

LANGUAGE IN ACTION

Present simple: affirmative and negative

I/you/we/they	*he/she/it*
Amir and his father **go** out in their boat.	Amir **lives** with his family.
They [1] *swim* in the water to look for food.	Amir [2] ________ a fish for breakfast.
Amir and his friends [3] ________ ________ to school.	He **doesn't know** his age.

Pronunciation p141

1 Complete the examples in the table above. Use the profile on page 24 to help you.

2 Correct the sentences. Check your answers in the profile on page 24.

1. Amir knows the date of his birthday.
   Amir doesn't know the date of his birthday.
2. He plays with his friends in the evenings.
   ____
3. He and his friends study English.
   ____
4. He and his friends don't like the water.
   ____
5. He doesn't have dinner with his family in the evenings.
   ____

3 Complete the text with the correct form of the present simple. Listen and check. 2.08

Nadia is 13 years old and she [1] *comes* (come) from Siberia. Her family is part of the Nenet tribe. They [2] ________ (not live) in the same place all year round. In summer, Nadia [3] ________ (travel) more than 1,000 km to the north of the country. She [4] ________ (not have got) a house. She [5] ________ (live) in a tent with her family. In winter, they [6] ________ (move) to the south of the country and their tent [7] ________ (go), too! How cool is that?

Adverbs of frequency

After breakfast, Amir [1] ________ meets his friends.
It's [2] ________ delicious.

4 Complete the examples in the table above. Use the profile on page 24 to help you.

5 Complete the timeline with the adverbs of frequency.

often sometimes usually

0%				100%
never	[1] ________	[2] ________	[3] ________	always

Use it!

6 Imagine you are a famous person. Write three positive and three negative sentences with adverbs of frequency about your daily routine. Use the ideas in the box.

do exercise do interviews have breakfast sing travel watch TV all afternoon

I always have breakfast in bed.

7 Swap your sentences with your partner. Guess who they are.

Are you Taylor Swift?

Yes, I am.

Finished? p119 Ex 2

VOCABULARY AND LISTENING

Leisure activities

2.09 **1 Match the activities in the box with the pictures. Listen, check and repeat.**

chat online	☐	download songs	☐
go for a bike ride	☐	go shopping	☐
hang out with friends	☐	listen to music	☐
make videos	☐	play an instrument	☐
play video games	☐	read a book/magazine	☐
take photos	☐	watch TV	1

LEARN TO LEARN

Word partners (2)

When you learn new words, learn them with the words that go with them. This will help you remember them.

2 Complete the table with the activities in Exercise 1.

	Leisure activities
Indoors	download songs ________ ________
Outdoors	
Indoors and outdoors	

3 Change the words in bold and write the correct the sentences.

1 I usually **chat** music on my phone.
I usually listen to music on my phone.

2 We never **read** videos.
____

3 Victor **listens to** photos all the time!
____

4 Alex **downloads** online with his friends every evening.
____

5 Evie and Laura **take** the piano together.
____

Street interviews

2.10 **4 Listen. Which activities from Exercise 1 do you hear?**

2.10 **5 Listen again. Circle the correct answers.**

1 Nina and her friends *like* / *don't like* the same music.
2 Nina *does* / *doesn't do* her homework before she chats online.
3 Anton *plays* / *doesn't play* video games on his own.
4 George *lives* / *doesn't live* near Anton.
5 Anton *has got* / *hasn't got* a bike and a camera.

Use it!

6 Write five sentences about your leisure activities. Use adverbs of frequency.

7 Work with a partner. Take turns to say your sentences. Are any the same?

I always chat online after school.

I never chat online after school. I read a magazine.

Watch video 2.3
Where does Sophie live?
What does Max make?

LANGUAGE IN ACTION

Present simple: questions

I/you/we/they	*he/she/it*
Do they **like** the same music?	[1] Does your best friend **live** near you?
Yes, they [2] ______ . / No, they **don't**.	Yes, he **does**. / No, he [3] ______ .
What [4] ______ you **do**?	**Who does** Anton **play** with?
How often [5] ______ you **chat** online?	**How often** [6] ______ she **do** that?

1 **Complete the examples in the table above.**

2 **Write the words in the correct order to make questions. Write the answers.**

1 Nina / hang out with friends / does ✓
Does Nina hang out with friends?
Yes, she does.

2 Nina and her friends / do / like / reading ✗
______
______

3 Nina / her homework / in the evenings / does / do ✓
______
______

4 Anton / walk / to George's house / does ✗
______
______

3 **Use the ideas to write questions. Ask and answer with a partner.**

1 play video games with friends (you)
Do you play video games with friends?
Yes, I do. / No, I don't.

2 live near you (your friends)
______
______

3 listen to music in the car (your parents)
______
______

4 get up early at the weekend (you)
______
______

Get it right!

Remember *do* and *does* in present simple questions.
Where does your best friend live? **NOT** ~~*Where your best friend live?*~~

Wh- questions

4 **Complete the questions with the words in the box.**

How often | What | What time | ~~When~~ | Where

1 When do you have breakfast?
2 ______ does your best friend live?
3 ______ do you get up on week days?
4 ______ do you do in your free time?
5 ______ does your English teacher give you homework?

Use it!

5 **Write questions. Ask and answer with a partner.**

1 What video games / you and your friends / like?
What video games do you and your friends like?

2 Where / your best friend / live?
______

3 Who / you / meet / before school?
______

What video games do you and your friends like?

I like adventure games, but my friends usually play football games.

Finished? p119 Ex 3

SPEAKING

An interview

1 2.11 **Listen to the conversation. Who is Mr Green?**

AMELIA	Hello, Mr Green. [1]*I've got some questions to ask you* for the school magazine. [2] ______ ?
MR GREEN	Go ahead.
AMELIA	What time do you get up in the morning?
MR GREEN	That's easy. I always get up at 5.30 am.
AMELIA	[3] ______ . So early! What time do you go to school?
MR GREEN	It depends. I usually arrive at about half past seven.
AMELIA	You're a history teacher here. Do you like your job?
MR GREEN	Good question! Of course I do, especially the interviews.
AMELIA	That's lucky!! [4] ______ .
MR GREEN	Sure!
AMELIA	What's your favourite day of the week?
MR GREEN	That's a difficult one! Saturday.
AMELIA	[5] ______ .
MR GREEN	No problem. You're welcome.

2 2.11 **Complete the conversation with the phrases from the *Useful language* box. Listen and check.**

Useful language

- I've got some questions to ask you.
- Is that OK?
- I've just got one more question.
- Thank you very much for your time.
- That's interesting.

3 **Look at the *Everyday English* box. Find and underline the phrases in the conversation.**

Watch video 2.4
Everyday English

Go ahead. It depends. No problem.
Sure! That's easy.

4 **Work with a partner. Practise the conversation.**

PLAN

5 **Work with a partner and decide who you want to interview. Write four questions that you want to ask. Use the ideas below. Decide on the person's answers.**

1 What time / get up?
What time do you get up in the morning?
I get up at 7.30 am.

2 What time / go to work?
______
______

3 Like job?
______
______

4 Favourite day?
______
______

SPEAK

6 **Practise the interview with your partner. Remember to use verbs in the present, the vocabulary from this unit and expressions from the *Useful language* and *Everyday English* boxes.**

CHECK

7 **Work with another pair. Listen to their interview and complete the notes.**

Who do they interview? ______
Favourite day: ______
Something interesting: ______
______

WRITING
An article

1 Read the article. Discuss the best title. Write it in the space in the article.

1 What do you do all day?
2 What's your daily routine?
3 What does a vlogger do all day?

2 Match topics a–c with paragraphs 1–3.

a Description of Amy's evening routine
b Description of her morning routine
c Description of her afternoon routine

3 Read the article again. What does Amy do at these times?

1 7.00 am She wakes up.
2 11.00 am ______
3 1.00 pm ______
4 9.00 pm ______

4 Look at the *Useful language* box. Write the punctuation used in 1–6.

1 I read a book. full stop
2 Close the door! ______
3 Do you chat online? ______
4 Canadian Amy Ritchie ______
5 chair, table, notebook ______
6 I'm they're don't ______

Useful language

apostrophe **'** capital letter **A, B, C**
comma **,** exclamation mark **!**
full stop **.** question mark **?**

5 Find and circle examples of the punctuation in the *Useful language* box in the article and title.

______

Amy Ritchie is a Canadian vlogger.
She vlogs about her life.

1 ☐ She always wakes up at 7.00, has breakfast and checks her phone. She plans her vlog but she doesn't make it. She usually goes for a bike ride at 11.00.

2 ☐ She has lunch at 1.00 and listens to music. Between 2.00 and 3.00, she practises her vlog. She takes some photos and posts them.

3 ☐ Amy doesn't have much free time. She sometimes watches TV before dinner. She always uploads her vlog at 9.00 pm and she goes to bed at 11.00.

One day I want to be a vlogger like Amy!

Write an article about daily activities.

PLAN

6 Choose a famous person. Think about their daily activities. Decide what information to include in each paragraph. Use the information in Exercise 2 to help you.

WRITE

7 Write your article. Remember to include the information in the correct order, the present simple, adverbs of frequency and correct punctuation from the *Useful language* box.

CHECK

8 Do you …

- include an interesting title with a question?
- introduce the person, their nationality and what they do?
- end the article with a sentence about you and your ambition?

Finished? p119 Ex 4

THE MATHS PROJECT

A class survey

1 **Circle the correct answer.**

A survey is a …

a test to check your knowledge.

b list of questions to find out information.

2.12 **2** **Look at the bar chart and complete the results of a class survey a–g. Listen and check.**

3 **Read the survey results again. Answer the questions.**

1 How many people are in the class? 30

2 What question do the students want to ask?

____

3 How do the students present the results?

____

4 What is the class's favourite leisure activity?

____

2.13 **4** **Complete the summary of the survey results with the words in the box. Listen and check.**

class ~~leisure~~ girls question results students surprising

2.13 **5** **Read the *How to* box and listen again. Answer the questions.**

1 Do the students complete each stage from the *How to* box?

____

2 What is the students' conclusion after the survey?

____

3 Do you think it is a good summary? Why / Why not?

____

How to present survey results

a Say what question you ask in your survey.

b Say why you want to do the survey.

c Give information about the people in the survey.

d Present the results.

e Give your opinion on the results.

f Comment on any surprising results.

g Summarise the survey results.

OUR CLASS SURVEY

SURVEY OF CLASS 7B: STUDENTS' LEISURE TIME

What do you do on Saturday mornings?

Total number of students: 30

a	hang out with friends	9
b	play video games	
c	go shopping	
d	watch TV	
e	listen to music	
f	stay in bed late	
g	tidy your bedroom	

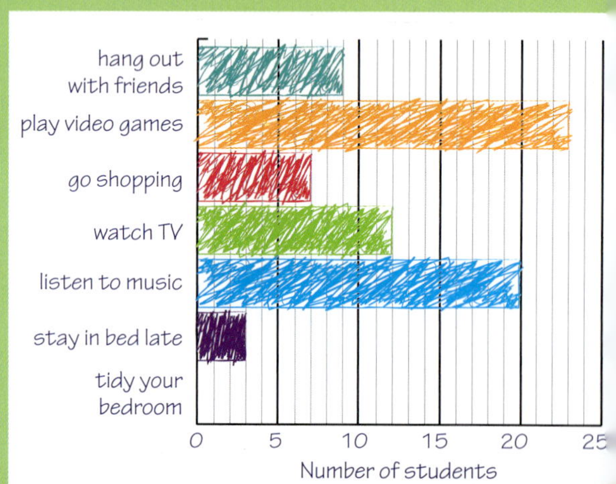

OWN IT!

Our survey is about [1] leisure activities on Saturday mornings. The purpose of our survey is to understand the leisure activities people do because we want to prepare an end of year party. It is good to know what people like!

Here are the results.

- There are 30 [2] ________ in our class. They are all between 12 and 13 years old. 16 are [3] ________ and 14 are boys.
- In response to the [4] ________ 'What do you do on Saturday mornings?' please look at the information in the chart.

- In our opinion, the [5] ________ are interesting. Students do a variety of different activities.
- Only three students stay in bed late on Saturday mornings. We think this is [6] ________ , because we know we're all tired after a week at school and we all like to sleep. Teenagers need between nine and ten hours sleep a night but we know leisure time is important for us, too.
- Most of the students in our [7] ________ play video games and no one tidies their bedroom on Saturday morning!

PLAN

6 Work in groups. Choose one of these topics. Complete the steps below.

Morning routines during the week

After-school activities

Evening activities

Weekend activities

- Decide on your question and the activities you want to include.
- Ask students your question and write down their answers.
- Add up the results.
- Draw a bar chart to show your results.

PRESENT

7 Present your results to the class. Remember to include carefully recorded information, an accurate bar chart and the tips in *How to* present survey results.

CHECK

8 Listen to your classmates' presentations and complete the notes.

What question do they ask?

____

What is their conclusion after the survey?

____

Write down two interesting or surprising facts.

____

____

2 REVIEW

VOCABULARY

1 Match the verbs with the activities.

1	brush	a	your bag
2	get	b	home
3	check	c	a shower
4	have	d	dressed
5	pack	e	your teeth
6	go	f	your phone

2 Circle the correct verb.

1 *play* / *go* / *chat* video games
2 *read* / *watch* / *make* a book
3 hang out with *music* / *friends* / *photos*
4 *listen to* / *go* / *chat* music
5 *chat* / *go* / *make* videos
6 *watch* / *take* / *listen to* photos

LANGUAGE IN ACTION

3 Complete the blog post with the correct form of the verbs. Use the present simple.

WELCOME TO

my morning routine!

My day [1] ______ (start) at 7.00 am during the week. I [2] ______ (wake up) but I [3] ______ (not get up). I [4] ______ (check) my phone. My best friend, Yusuf, always [5] ______ (send) me a photo in the morning. He's funny! Breakfast is at 7.30. Then my sister and I [6] ______ (pack) our bags for school.

I [7] ______ (not meet) Yusuf in the morning because he [8] ______ (not go) to my school.

What's your morning routine like?

4 Write questions. Answer the questions for you.

1 your best friend / play an instrument?

2 how often / you / watch / TV?

3 what / your friends / do / at the weekend?

4 what time / school / start / in the morning?

5 where / you / hang out / with friends?

6 how often / you / go / for a bike ride?

5 Put the words in the correct order to make sentences.

1 watch / never / we / before school / TV

2 chats / sometimes / she / online

3 shopping / they / at the weekend / go / often

4 music / bedroom / I / my / listen to / usually / in

Self-assessment

I can talk about my daily routine.

I can talk about my leisure activities.

I can use the present simple in affirmative and negative sentences.

I can use the present simple to ask questions.

LEARN TO ... WORK IN PAIRS

When you work in pairs, you learn from your partner.

1 **Complete the advice 1–6 with *Always* or *Never*.**

Let's work well together!

1 Always listen to your partner.

2 ______ answer your partner's questions.

3 ______ speak at the same time as your partner.

4 ______ help your partner with words they don't know.

5 ______ laugh at your partner's mistakes.

6 ______ ask questions to get more information.

OWN IT!

2 **Ask and answer questions with a partner. Complete sentences 1–4. Practise the advice in Exercise 1.**

1 We both like ______.

2 My partner likes ______ but I don't.

3 I like ______ but my partner doesn't.

4 We don't like ______.

Do you like hanging out with friends?

Yes, I do.

Me, too. Let's write 'hanging out with friends' in sentence 1.

3 **Complete the sentences about how you work in pairs with *always*, *sometimes* or *never*.**

When I work in pairs …

1 I always listen to my partner.

2 I ______ answer my partner's questions.

3 I ______ speak at the same time as my partner.

4 I ______ help my partner with words they don't know.

5 I ______ laugh at my partner's mistakes.

6 I ______ ask questions to get more information.

4 **Tell your partner your sentences from Exercise 3. Do they agree? Why / Why not?**

I always listen to my partner.

Hmm. You sometimes listen to your partner.

3 SCHOOL DAYS

LEARNING OUTCOMES

I can ...

- understand texts about schools and school activities
- learn how to ask for help
- write a description of my ideal school
- understand how to use *can/can't* and *like*, *love*, etc. + *-ing*
- talk about school subjects and places in a school
- recognise cognates, make a spidergram and understand new words from context.

Start it!

1 Look at the photo. How is this classroom different to your classroom?
2 Before you watch, how do you go to school?
3 Where do the students have their lessons? Watch and check.
4 Which school do you want to go to? Why?

Watch video 3.1

p37

Language in action 3.2

p39

Language in action 3.3

p40

Everyday English 3.4

p42

Globetrotters 3.5

VOCABULARY
School subjects

1 (3.01) **Match the school subjects with the pictures. Listen, check and repeat.**

art ☐ design and technology (DT) ☐
drama ☐ English ☐ food technology ☐
geography ☐ history ☐
information and communication technology (ICT) ☐
maths [a] music ☐
physical education (PE) ☐
science ☐ Spanish ☐

2 **Circle the correct subjects.**

1 *Maths* / *Art* is my favourite subject. I love difficult sums.
2 I don't like *PE* / *food technology* when we go outside. I prefer it inside.
3 This year I want to study Shakespeare in *science* / *English*.
4 I never remember all the dates in *history* / *ICT*.
5 *Geography* / *English* isn't just about countries. It's also about population and people.
6 *Music* / *Spanish* is great this year. My word of the week is *gracias*.

3 **Work with a partner. Ask and answer about your timetables. Talk about:**

subjects you're good at
your favourite subjects
subjects you're not good at
good/bad days

I'm good at PE. I'm not good at art. What about you?

LEARN TO LEARN
Recognising cognates

Some English words are similar to words in your language, but we don't always use them in the same way.

4 **Write the subjects from Exercise 1 under the headings. Can you add any more subjects?**

Similar to the names of subjects in my language	Very different from the names of subjects in my language

Use it!

5 **Write five definitions for school subjects. Can your partner guess the subjects?**

You draw and paint in this subject. *Art!*

Explore it!

Guess the correct answer.

In Australia, students have six weeks' *summer* / *winter* holiday from mid-December to the end of January.

Find an interesting fact about schools. Write a question for your partner to answer.

READING
A webpage

Ballet School

Rumba, mambo, and salsa are just some of the dance styles that come from Cuba, and dancers are big stars in Cuba. The Cuban National Ballet School in Havana **trains** boys and girls to do **ballet** and many of the students become the world's **top** ballet dancers.

Children usually start at the school when they are ten years old, for five years of training. Then they sometimes train for three and a half more years at a professional level.

The school day starts at 7.00 am and finishes at 7.00 pm. That's a 12-hour day! And some students go to school before classes start to do exercises! In the morning students study subjects like history, maths, languages, science and music. At lunchtime they can have a break, but they can't go home. In the afternoons, they dance.

Oscar is a student there. 'It's **tough** and sometimes I just want to do nothing. I can dance and read music quite well, but I can't play the piano at all. My best friend Carlos can dance very well. He can sing well, too, but I can't – I sing badly! One day, I want to be a dancer like my **hero**, Javier Rojas.'

Learning to be a top ballet dancer is really hard work! Are you tough enough?

1 **Look at the photo and read the title. What do you want to know about the webpage?**

3.02 **2** **Read the webpage. Close your books. Write two things you remember about it.**

3 **Find the words in bold in the webpage. Circle the correct option.**

1. Train is to *prepare yourself for* / *think about* an activity.
2. Ballet *isn't* / *is* a type of dance.
3. Top is to be number *one* / *two*.
4. Tough is something *easy* / *difficult*.
5. Hero is a person you think is *great* / *not very good*.

4 **Read the webpage again and complete the sentences.**

1. The Cuban National Ballet School is in ____Havana____ .
2. Lots of the students become world-famous ________ .
3. Most students start training at the school when they are ________ .
4. Some students ________ in the morning before classes start.
5. Students can have a break at ________ .
6. In the afternoons, students ________ .

Voice it!

5 **Discuss the questions.**

1. Has your country got schools like Oscar's school? What type?
2. What are the similarities and the differences between your school and Oscar's?
3. Do you want to go to a ballet school like Oscar? Why / Why not?

Finished? p120 Ex 1

Watch video 3.2
Can he speak another language?
Can anyone become a vlogger?

LANGUAGE IN ACTION
can for ability and permission

I/you/he/she/it/we/they	
Ability	**Permission**
I [1] *can* dance.	At lunchtime they [2] ______ have a break.
Oscar **can't** play the piano.	Students [3] ______ go home at lunchtime.
Can Oscar sing well? Yes, he **can**. / No, he **can't**.	**Can** they dance here? Yes, they **can**. / No, they **can't**.

Pronunciation p141

1 **Complete the examples in the table above. Use the webpage on page 36 to help you.**

2 **Circle the correct option. Check your answers in the webpage on page 36.**

1 Oscar *can* (circled) / *can't* read music.
2 Oscar *can* / *can't* sing well.
3 Carlos *can* / *can't* sing well.
4 Javier Rojas *can* / *can't* dance well.

3.06 **3** **Complete the text with the correct form of *can*. Listen and check.**

Get it right!

We use the verb without *to* after *can*.
Vicki can sing **NOT** ~~*Vicki can to sing*~~

A day in Huaho school

Huaho school in Finland is different. Can you guess why?

Students [1] *can choose* (choose) the subjects they want to study. Teachers [2] ______ (tell) them what to do. Students [3] ______ (use) their mobiles in class to do research.

[4] ______ (you / do) that in your school?

Students and teachers [5] ______ (take) a break after every lesson. They [6] ______ (chat) to friends or go outside.

Students [7] ______ (do) homework. Why? Because the teachers don't give them any!

[8] ______ (you / imagine) a school like this?

4 **Remember the information from the webpage and complete the sentences.**

☺☺☺ very well ☺☺ well ☺ quite well
☹☹☹ at all ☹☹ badly ☹ not very well

1 Oscar can read music ______ .
2 He can't play the piano ______ .
3 Carlos can dance ______ .
4 Oscar can sing ______ .

Use it!

5 **Write sentences about things you can or can't do and how well or badly you do them. Use the ideas below or your own ideas.**

count to ten in a different language do ballet
sing a song in Russian write music

I can't do ballet at all but I can dance well.

6 **Ask and answer questions. Find one thing you and your partner can both do well and one thing you can't do at all.**

Can you count to ten in a different language?

Yes, I can. I can count to ten in English very well.

Finished? p120 Ex 2

VOCABULARY AND LISTENING

Places in a school

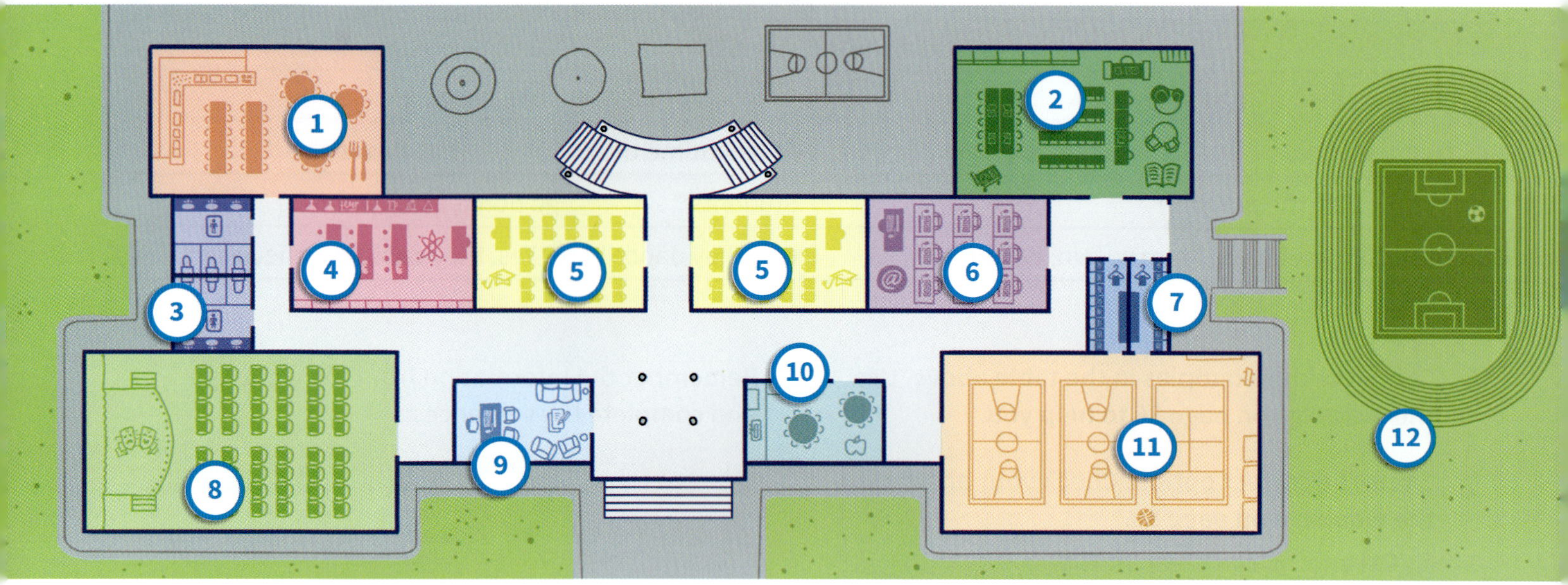

3.07 **1 Match the words with places 1–12 in the plan. Listen, check and repeat.**

canteen	1	classroom		ICT room	
library		locker area		main hall	
playing field		reception		science lab	
sports hall		staffroom		toilets	

3.08 **2 Listen and write the seven places you hear.**

1 ______
2 ______
3 ______
4 ______
5 ______
6 ______
7 ______

LEARN TO LEARN

Making a spidergram

Try to think of other words related to new words and make spidergrams to increase your vocabulary.

3 Choose places in your school from Exercise 1. Write down other words related to them.

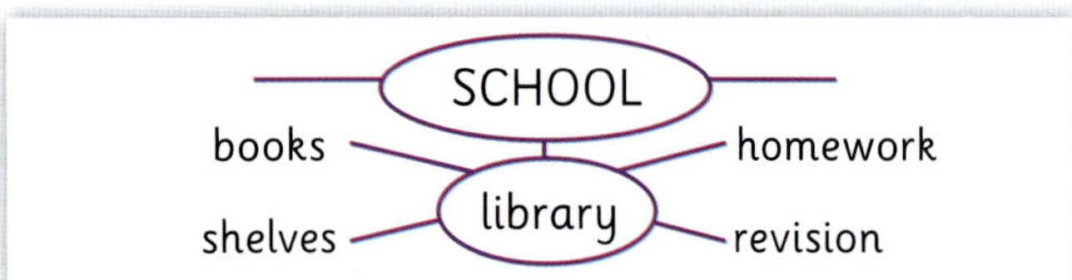

Use it!

4 Ask and answer about the places in your school. Use as many words as you can from Exercises 1 and 3.

Where do you do homework?

I do my homework in the library. What about you?

A radio programme

3.09 **5 Listen. What is the radio programme about?**

3.09 **6 Listen again. Circle the correct answers.**

1 The club is usually in the *main hall* / *library*.
2 The club meets once a *week* / *month*.
3 The club *starts* / *finishes* at 3.15.
4 Mrs McKenzie is Lidia's *drama* / *English* teacher.
5 Max lives *near* / *far from* the school.

Voice it!

7 Discuss the questions.

1 What kinds of books do you like?
2 Have you got a book club at your school?
3 Which clubs do you go to? When and where are they?

LANGUAGE IN ACTION

Verb forms: *(don't) like, don't mind, love, hate + -ing*

Watch video 3.3
What's her favourite subject?
What does she love doing?

We all **love reading** books. ☺☺☺	I **don't mind staying** for the book club. 😐
We **like** [1]**talk**ing ______ about them, too. ☺	I [2] ______ **like going** to after-school clubs. ☹
Some of my friends **hate** [3]**read** ______ . ☹☹☹	

1 Complete the examples in the table above.

2 Complete the sentences. Which ones are correct (✓)?

1 Lidia loves reading (read) books. ☺☺☺ ✓
2 The students at the book club ______ (talk) about books. ☹ ☐
3 Max usually ______ (go) to after-school clubs. ☹☹☹ ☐
4 Max ______ (stay) for this club. 😐 ☐
5 All of Max's friends ______ (read). ☺ ☐

3 Write true sentences. Use the ideas in the box or your own ideas.

do homework with friends	get up early
hang out with friends	learn new vocabulary
listen to rap music	read a book
revise for exams	take photos

I like doing homework with friends.

4 Ask and answer. Find three things you have in common.

Do you like getting up early?

No! I hate getting up early. What about you?

I don't mind getting up early on week days.

Object pronouns

We use object pronouns after a verb or preposition to replace nouns and to avoid repeating the same word.

5 Match the object pronouns with the people or things.

1 Lidia's here with **me**.
2 We like talking about **them**, too!
3 We have English with **her**.
4 What's **it** about?

a books
b the radio presenter
c Lidia's book
d Mrs McKenzie

6 Complete the sentences.

1 Is Logan in this class? I want to talk to him .
2 Our teacher always gives ______ a lot of homework.
3 Where are Jess and Mehmet? Let's call ______ now.
4 The seat next to Ava is free. You can sit next to ______ .
5 Is this your dictionary? Can I borrow ______ , please?

Use it!

7 Think about things you like and don't like at your school. Compare your ideas with a partner. Agree on changes you want to make.

I don't like eating in the canteen. The food isn't good.

I agree. Let's change our routine on Mondays. We can cook lunch at home at the weekend and bring it to school.

8 Present your favourite idea to the class with your partner. The class chooses the best idea.

Finished? p120 Ex 3

SPEAKING
Asking for help

3.10 **1 Listen to the conversation. What is Leo's problem?**

LEO Hi, Nora. How's it going?
NORA Not bad, thanks. You?
LEO Not great. I can't do my maths project. I'm stuck!
NORA Not again! Oh dear.
LEO [1] Can you help me ____, please?
NORA What's the problem?
LEO I hate working out survey results. I can't do it.
NORA Don't be silly! Of course you can. [2] __________ the results?
LEO Yes, please.
NORA Go on then.
LEO Thanks. [3] __________? I don't mind doing the bar chart. I can do that!
NORA Of course I'm sure. Can you do [4] __________ now?
LEO Sure.
NORA Stop talking about maths and let's go for lunch!

3.10 **2 Complete the conversation with the phrases from the *Useful language* box. Listen and check.**

Useful language

Are you sure?
Can you do me a favour?
Can you help me, please?
Do you need a hand with …?

3 Look at the *Everyday English* box. Find and underline the phrases in the conversation.

Watch video 3.4
Everyday English

Don't be silly! I'm stuck.
Not again! Not great. Oh dear!

4 Work with a partner. Practise the conversation.

PLAN

5 Work with a partner. Decide what the problem is and what help you need. Use the ideas below or your own ideas.

a school project your (maths/drama, etc.) homework
a science experiment

SPEAK

6 Practise the conversation asking for help with your partner. Remember to use *can/can't* and *(don't) like, don't mind, love, hate* + *-ing*. Also use the vocabulary from this unit and expressions from the *Useful language* and *Everyday English* boxes.

CHECK

7 Work with another pair. Listen to their conversation and complete the notes.

What is the problem? __________
____
What help do they need? __________
____
What is the solution to the problem? __________
____

WRITING
A description

1 Read Azra's description. Do you think *Dream Academy* is a real school? Why / Why not?

Dream Academy

I'm a student at Dream Academy.

1 ☐
Students can study traditional subjects like maths and English. They can also study 'how to' subjects such as how to make videos, record and produce music, be a photographer, be a DJ. My favourite subject is how to be a DJ!

2 ☐
Students choose their own teachers. They interview them and decide together. For example, the music teacher is a famous pop star.

3 ☐
Students never have more than four lessons a day. Students can choose when lessons start and finish.

4 ☐
Students don't have lessons in classrooms – they are in learning pods. My favourite space is the music pod. I love listening to music in it.

I love studying at Dream Academy.

Azra

2 **Match headings a–d with paragraphs 1–4.**

a Only four lessons
b Creative spaces
c Amazing subjects
d Star teachers

3 **Read the *Useful language* box. Find and <u>underline</u> sentences with these words in Azra's description.**

Useful language

for example like such as

Write a description of your ideal school.

PLAN

4 **Make a spidergram about your ideal school.**

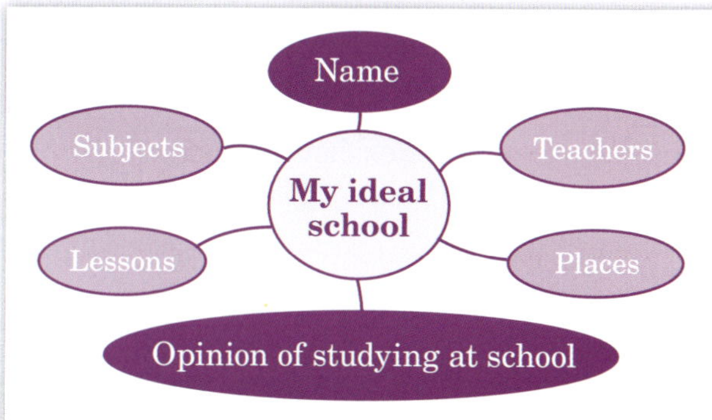

Decide what information to include in each paragraph of your description. Use your spidergram and the information in Exercise 2 to help you.

WRITE

5 **Write your description. Remember to include four paragraphs, *can/can't* and expressions from the *Useful language* box.**

CHECK

6 **Do you …**

- give the name of the school in the opening sentence?
- include all of the information from your spidergram?
- give your opinion about studying at the school in your closing sentence?

Finished? p120 Ex 4

AROUND THE WORLD

READING
A blog post

Globetrotters
Watch video 3.5
The School of the Air

- Where is Jamie and Paul's school?
- What subjects do they study?
- What do Jamie and Paul love doing?

3.11 **1** **Write three things you want to know about school life in Japan. Compare with a partner. Read the blog. Does it answer your questions?**

2 **Read the blog again and answer the questions.**

1. What does Hideki do when he gets to school?
   He takes off his shoes and puts them in his locker.
2. How often do the students have an assembly?
   ______
3. Where does Hideki have lunch?
   ______
4. What do the students do at 3.30?
   ______
5. How many hours does Hideki spend at school?
   ______

3 **Find and underline words in the blog to match the definitions.**

1. Paragraph 1 (adj) for wearing or doing outside; not inside a building
2. Paragraph 5 (n) letters or numbers you use when you write
3. Paragraph 6 (n) something you play with small pieces, for example, chess

Voice it!

4 **Discuss the questions.**

1. What is respect? Why is it important?
2. How does Hideki show his teachers respect?
3. Can you give an example of when you show respect?

Welcome to my school day!

My school day starts at 8.30 am. When I arrive, I take off my shoes and I put them in my locker. We can't wear outdoor shoes at school so we put on special **indoor** shoes.

We have an assembly with the principal in the main hall on Monday mornings and we have six 50-minute classes every day. My best subjects are Japanese, science and art.

Lunchtime starts at 12.30 pm. We don't eat lunch in a canteen – we stay in our classroom. Different students **serve** the meal every day and a teacher eats with us.

When classes end at 3.30, we all stay to clean and tidy up the classrooms and throw away the **rubbish**. I don't mind doing these jobs. It's an important part of school life and I like having the responsibility.

Nearly everyone belongs to an after-school club. One of my clubs meets on Mondays and Thursdays to learn about traditional Japanese arts like Shodo and Haiku. Haiku is a type of Japanese poetry. Shodo is writing Japanese characters *(kanji)*. I can write some characters quite well now.

My other club is the *Go* club. It's on Tuesdays and Fridays. *Go* is a Japanese board game and it's more than 2,500 years old. I love playing it, but when I leave school after a long, busy day at 5.30 I'm usually **exhausted**.

LEARN TO LEARN

Understanding new words from context

When you read a text, don't look up every word. Find other words you know in the same sentence and try to guess the meaning of the new word.

5 **Look at the words in bold in the blog. What do they mean? Which other words in the sentences do you know?**

6 **Find and circle these phrasal verbs in the text. What do they mean?**

put on	take off	throw away	tidy up

7 **Complete the sentences with the phrasal verbs from Exercise 6.**

1. It's hot in here. __________ your coat!
2. Now it's cold. Can I __________ my coat again?
3. I can help you to __________ your room. We can __________ all the rubbish.

Explore it!

Is the sentence *T* (true) or *F* (false)?

Japanese teachers and students work even during the holidays! ☐

Find three more interesting facts about school life in Japan. Choose your favourite fact and write a question for your partner to answer.

OWN IT! The Culture Project Teacher's Resource Bank

3 REVIEW

VOCABULARY

1 Write the school subjects.

1  ____________

2  ____________

3 

____

4  ____________

5  ____________

6 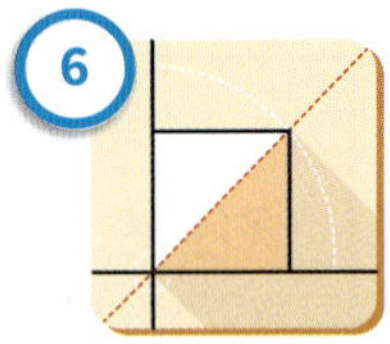 ____________

7  ____________

8  ____________

9  ____________

2 Read the sentences and write the places.

1 Teachers go here at break. ____________
2 Students do experiments here. ____________
3 Students choose books here. ____________
4 We have lunch here. ____________
5 We always go here for an assembly. ____________

LANGUAGE IN ACTION

3 Answer the questions. Write sentences that are true for you.

How well can you …

1 speak English?
____
2 use a computer?
____
3 do difficult maths problems?
____
4 cook?
____
5 dance?
____

4 Write questions and short answers. Use *can*.

1 Jack / ride a bike? (✓)
____
____
2 Layla / sing well? (✗)
____
____
3 your grandma and grandad / use a computer (✓)
____
____
4 we / drive a car? (✗)
____
____

5 Complete the sentences with the correct object pronouns.

1 We can't do this. Can you help ____________?
2 Is that James? I'm not sure it's ____________.
3 Where's my phone? Have you got ____________?
4 Liz is stuck. Can you give ____________ a hand?

6 Write the sentences.

1 She / love / do / maths every day
____
2 We / not mind / get up / early / for school
____
3 They / hate / play / football
____
4 He / not like / revise / for exams
____

Self-assessment

I can talk about my school subjects.
I can talk about the places in my school.
I can use *can* and *can't* to talk about ability and permission.
I can use verbs to talk about what I do and don't like doing.

LEARN TO LEARN

LEARN TO ... USE FLASHCARDS

Flashcards can help you remember new vocabulary.

1 Match the front and back of the flashcards.

1 information and ______ technology (ICT)

2 

3 hang ______ with friends

4 a place where you do experiments

5 

a science lab

b glasses

c moustache

d communication

e out

2 Tick the types of flashcard you can see in Exercise 1.

1 ☑ picture + word
2 ☐ phrase with one word missing
3 ☐ word in English + word in your language
4 ☐ word + meaning
5 ☐ word + example sentence

3 Choose five words or phrases from Unit 3. Use the words or phrases to make the five different types of flashcards in Exercise 2.

OWN IT!

4 Show the front of your flashcards from Exercise 3 to your partner. Can they guess what is on the back of each flashcard?

physical ______

Physical ... Oh, I don't know!

It's a school subject.

Physical education!

Yes! That's right!

5 Discuss with your partner. Which is your favourite type of flashcard from Exercise 2? Why?

4 YOU ARE WHAT YOU EAT

LEARNING OUTCOMES

I can ...

- understand texts about food
- order in a snack bar
- write a description of my favourite food
- understand how to use countable and uncountable nouns and *there is/are*
- talk about and describe food
- personalise vocabulary and answer true/false questions
- design a food truck and evaluate a design project.

Start it!

1 Look at the picture. what can you see?
2 Before you watch, name three types of food.
3 How can you learn to cook? Watch and check.
4 Do you like cooking?

Watch video 4.1

p49

Language in action 4.2

p51

Language in action 4.3

p52

Everyday English 4.4

VOCABULARY
Food and drink

1 **Write all the food and drink words you know in English. Compare with a partner.**

4.01 **2** **Match the words in the box with the photos. Listen, check and repeat.**

apples	☐	bananas	☐	beans	☐
carrots	☐	cheese	☐	chicken	☐
chocolate	a	eggs	☐	fish	☐
fizzy drink	☐	juice	☐	meat	☐
rice	☐	water	☐		

LEARN TO LEARN
Personalising vocabulary
Think about your own routines and habits when you learn new vocabulary.

3 **When do you have the food and drinks in Exercise 2? Write the words in the table.**

Breakfast	Lunch	Dinner

4 **Compare with a partner. Write sentences about your partner's meals. Use adverbs of frequency.**

Eva always has an egg and juice for breakfast.

Get it right!

We say *I don't like apples.* **NOT** ~~*I don't like the apples.*~~

Use it!

5 **Discuss the questions.**

1 Which food do you love/hate?

2 Which food do you eat when you're happy? What about when you're sad?

Explore it!

Guess the correct answer.

One hundred grams of ants have got …

a less protein than an egg.

b more protein than an egg.

c the same protein as an egg.

Find an interesting fact about food. Write a question for your partner to answer.

Time for a snack

a  

Leakena is from Cambodia. She hasn't got a banana for a snack today, she's got a spider. She usually buys one tarantula from a food stall on the way home from school. 'You cook them in **oil** and then add some **salt** and some sugar. They're like chicken or fish. The legs are my favourite!'

b  

Kgosi is from Botswana in southern Africa. He hasn't got any apples today, but he's got some Mopane worms. 'I like sharing them with friends at school. They're great with some **peanut butter** or some rice and they've got more protein than meat. I haven't got any rice today, just 50 worms!'

c  

Jorge is from Oaxaca, Mexico. He's got some chocolate today but he's also got a grasshopper taco. 'My mum cooks grasshoppers in some oil and she always adds some **garlic**. They're my favourite snack and I sometimes buy them at the market'. Bugs like grasshoppers, spiders, and worms are good for you and the planet. They give us protein and they aren't expensive to feed. Which bug do you want to try?

READING
An article

1 **Look at the photos of food in the article. Where do you think people eat this food? Do they enjoy it?**

4.02 **2** **Read the article and check your answers to Exercise 1.**

3 **Check the meaning of the words in bold in the article.**

4 **Choose the correct answer. Which person ...**

Leakena Kgosi Jorge

1 enjoys sharing snacks with friends? Kgosi
2 usually buys a snack after school? ______
3 enjoys the snack with garlic and oil? ______
4 likes eating the snack with rice? ______
5 has got two types of snack today? ______
6 likes eating a bug's legs? ______

Voice it!

5 **Discuss the questions.**

1 Do people in your country eat bugs?
2 Which of these bugs do you want to try?
3 Why do you think eating bugs is good for the planet?

Finished? p121 Ex 1

Watch video 4.2
What food can you see at the market?
What's his favourite food?

LANGUAGE IN ACTION
Countable and uncountable nouns

Countable nouns	Uncountable nouns
Some nouns are countable: you can count them. *one tarantula, 50 worms, a taco, an apple*	Other nouns are uncountable: you can't count them. *chocolate, salt, sugar, meat, garlic*

1 **Complete the table with the food words in the box.**

~~beans~~ bread carrots cheese eggs fish juice meat milk rice tomatoes

Countable		Uncountable	
beans	______	______	______
______	______	______	______
______	______	______	______
______	______	______	______
______	______	______	______
______	______	______	______

2 **Work with a partner. Add more food words to the table in Exercise 1. How many have you got?**

a/an, some/any

Singular countable	Plural countable	Uncountable
Leakena's got [1] *a* spider.	Kgosi's got [2] ______ worms.	Jorge's got [3] ______ chocolate today.
She hasn't got [4] ______ banana.	He hasn't got [5] ______ apples.	Kgosi hasn't got [6] ______ rice today.
Have you got **a** spider?	Have you got **any** worms?	Have you got **any** chocolate?

3 **Complete the examples in the table above. Use the article on page 48 to help you.**

4.03 **4** **Complete the conversation with *a*, *an*, *some* or *any*. Listen and check.**

CELIA Have we got [1] *any* food for the party?
OSCAR Let's have a look. Right, we've got [2] ______ cheese.
CELIA OK. Have we got [3] ______ bread?
OSCAR Sorry. We haven't got [4] ______ bread but we've got [5] ______ pasta.
CELIA Have we got [6] ______ fruit or vegetables?
OSCAR We've got [7] ______ apple and [8] ______ carrot.
CELIA What about drinks?
OSCAR We've got [9] ______ water.
CELIA Great. What a party! I can't wait.

Use it!

5 **Work with a partner. Change the food and drink words in Exercise 4 and write your own conversation. Practise your conversation.**

6 **Listen carefully to other conversations. Which party do you want to go to?**

Finished? p121 Ex 2

VOCABULARY AND LISTENING

Adjectives

4.04 **1** Complete the sentences with the adjectives in the box. Listen and check.

cold delicious disgusting fresh healthy hot nice salty sweet ~~unhealthy~~

1 *Fizzy drinks aren't good for you, but I sometimes drink them. I know they're* unhealthy.

2 *Careful! The soup is ________.*

3 *Peanuts have got salt on them. They're ________, but they aren't bad for you.*

4 *I really hate cheese. I don't know how people can eat it, I think it's ________.*

5 *These beetles look and taste great! They're ________.*

6 *Yuk! This milk doesn't smell ________. I don't want any in my coffee.*

7 *Dark chocolate hasn't got much sugar in it. It isn't ________, but I love it!*

8 *I never eat ice cream in winter. The weather is ________ and so is ice cream!*

9 *The vegetables and fruit in our garden are always ________ and they're a ________ snack.*

4.05 **2** Listen to the words in Exercise 1 and repeat them. Which two words have got a negative meaning?

> Pronunciation p141

Use it!

3 Write five sentences to describe a type of food. Use adjectives.

4 Work with a partner. Take turns to say your sentences. Can your partner guess the type of food?

They're disgusting and salty.

Are they spiders?

A quiz

LEARN TO LEARN

True or false sentences

With true or false sentences, you've got a 50% chance of being correct! Before you listen, read the sentences and try to predict if they are true or false.

5 Read the sentences in Exercise 6 and predict if they are *T* (true) or *F* (false).

4.08 **6** Listen to the quiz and check. How many of your predictions are correct?

1 There are 1,000 peanuts in a jar of peanut butter. ___
2 You can't eat durians on public transport. ___
3 White chocolate isn't really chocolate. ___
4 Carmine is an orange powder from beetles. ___

durian

cocoa

carmine

Watch video 4.3
What is in her juice?
How many hours does she sleep?

LANGUAGE IN ACTION

there is/isn't, there are/aren't

Countable singular	Uncountable	Countable plural
There's a quiz in this magazine.	**There's** some water in the fridge.	**There are** 540 peanuts in a jar.
There isn't a quiz in the magazine.	**There** [1] isn't any water.	**There aren't** any oranges in this drink.
Is there a quiz in the magazine?	**Is** [2] ______ any water?	**Are** [3] ______ five questions in the quiz?
Yes, there is. / **No, there isn't.**	**Yes,** [4] ______ ______. / **No,** [5] ______ ______.	**Yes, there are.** / **No,** [6] ______ ______.

1 Complete the examples in the table above.

2 Circle the correct words. Listen and check. 4.09

ALI I'm hungry! Let's make some chicken and rice.
BEN We can't! There [1]*is* / *isn't* any rice.
ALI OK. What about an omelette? [2]*There are* / *Are there* any eggs?
BEN [3]*There's* / *There are* only one!
ALI Oh dear! [4]*There is* / *Is there* any pasta?
BEN No, there [5]*is* / *isn't*.
ALI [6]*Is* / *Are* there any potatoes? Let's make chips!
BEN No, there [7]*are* / *aren't*. There [8]*isn't* / *aren't* any food in the house!
ALI [9]*There's* / *There are* a food market today. Let's go!
BEN OK. Oh no – I haven't got any money!

3 Write questions about the picture.

1 any fruit? Is there any fruit?
2 any eggs? ______
3 any juice? ______
4 a sandwich? ______

4 Ask and answer the questions in Exercise 3.

Is there any fruit?

Yes, there is.

much/many, a lot of

Countable plural	Uncountable
There are **a lot of** peanuts.	I've got **a** [1] ______ **of** homework.
There aren't **many** questions.	I haven't got **much** time.
How [2] ______ questions are there?	**How** [3] ______ time have you got?

5 Complete the examples in the table above.

Use it!

6 Write questions with *how much/how many*.

1 fruit / do you eat / every day?
How much fruit do you eat every day?
2 people / are there / in your family?
______
3 books / do you read / in a year?
______
4 time / spend / with friends at the weekend?
______

7 Ask and answer the questions in Exercise 6.

How much fruit do you eat every day?

I eat an apple and an orange.

Finished? p121 Ex 3

SPEAKING
Ordering food and drink

1 (4.10) **Listen to the conversation. What does Gulay choose from The Juice Stop?**

JUST JUICES: £4.00

THE JUICE STOP
Fresh and Natural

Sunshine Start
Start your day with a delicious mix of fruit and vegetables.

Green Giant
Gives you energy with fresh green vegetables and there's an apple, too!

Fresh Lemorange
3 oranges, 2 lemons, some fizzy water and our secret ingredient.

WATER STOP: £1.50
Fizzy water

SNACK STATION: £0.75
Apple, Banana, Carrot

SERVER	Hi. [1] *Can I help you* ?
GULAY	[2] ________ juice, please.
SERVER	No problem. [3] ________ ?
GULAY	I'm not sure. [4] ________ Sunshine Start?
SERVER	There are two oranges, a carrot and three tomatoes in that one. It's really healthy.
GULAY	Hmm. What about the Green Giant? That sounds delicious.
SERVER	There are some green beans and a green apple in that.
GULAY	Thanks. [5] ________ some fizzy water and an apple?
SERVER	Of course. No worries! [6] ________ ?
GULAY	Yes, it is. Thank you. [7] ________ ?
SERVER	[8] ________ £2.25, ________ .
GULAY	Here you go.
SERVER	Thanks. Enjoy!
GULAY	Thank you. Bye!

2 (4.10) **Complete the conversation with the phrases from the *Useful language* box. Listen and check.**

Useful language

Can I have … ?	Is that everything?
Can I help you?	That's … , please.
How much is that?	What kind?
I'd like a/an/some …	What's in the … ?

3 **Look at the *Everyday English* box. Find and <u>underline</u> the phrases in the conversation.**

Watch video 4.4
Everyday English

Enjoy! Here you go.
No problem. No worries!

4 **Work with a partner. Practise the conversation.**

PLAN

5 **Work with a partner. Plan a conversation about ordering food and drink. Decide …**

where you are ________
who is the server and who is the customer ________
what's on the menu ________
how much money the customer has got ________
what to choose from the menu ________

SPEAK

6 **Practise the conversation. Remember to use *there is(n't)* / *there are(n't)* and *how much* / *how many*. Also use the vocabulary from this unit and expressions from the *Useful language* and *Everyday English* boxes.**

CHECK

7 **Work with another pair. Listen to their conversation and complete the notes.**

Where are they? ________
What does the customer choose from the menu? ________

WRITING
A description

My favourite food

by João Pereira

1 ☐ My name's João and I'm from Recife in Brazil. Here are some photos of my favourite types of food. I often have these at the weekend.

2 ☐ My dad makes cheese bread for breakfast. There's a lot of cheese in it. It's nice and I eat it when it's hot!

3 ☐ I usually buy lunch from a food stall or a shop. There are a lot of food stalls in my part of town and it isn't difficult to find delicious food! We often have chicken xim xim. It's very healthy. It's chicken with rice and there are a lot of peanuts. They're salty but they're nice.

4 ☐ I love chocolate balls. I always buy them after lunch from Thiago's stall. They're very sweet. I love eating them with my hands but I can't eat more than two or three. They're definitely my favourite snack!

1 **Look at the photos. What do you think the food is? Read the description and check.**

2 **Match topics a–d with paragraphs 1–4.**

- a Snacks
- b Introduction: who you are, what the description is about
- c Breakfast
- d Lunch

3 **Find and underline examples of *and*, *but* and *or* in João's description. Complete the information in the *Useful language* box.**

Useful language

We use [1] ______ to add similar information.
We use [2] ______ to contrast different information.
We use [3] ______ when there is a choice (usually between two things).

Write a description of your favourite types of food.

PLAN

4 **Make notes to describe your favourite types of food. Say where you get it from, what's in it and what it's like. Decide what information to include in each paragraph. Use the information in Exercise 2 to help you.**

WRITE

5 **Write your description. Remember to include four paragraphs, *there is/are*, countable and uncountable nouns and expressions from the *Useful language* box.**

CHECK

6 **Do you ...**

- introduce yourself and say when/how often you eat your favourite foods?
- use adjectives to describe food?
- say why you like each type of food?

Finished? p121 Ex 4

THE ART PROJECT

Design a food truck

1 Discuss the questions.

1 What food do you buy in the street or from food trucks?
2 When do people buy food from a food truck?
3 Are there any food trucks near where you live?

2 Look at the food truck and answer the questions.

1 What kind of food do you think it sells? Caribbean food.
2 What kind of soup is there? ______
3 How much does today's special cost? ______
4 What sweet food can you buy? ______
5 What is the special offer? ______

3 Work with a partner. Choose the food you want to order from the food truck. Compare with another pair.

How to evaluate a design

4.11 **4 What do you think are the most important things in a design project? Circle the things in the list. Listen and check.**

a design
b content
c punctuation
d grammar
e paragraphs
f spelling

5 How well do you think the *Caribbean Sunshine* project presents the things in the table? Use the key to evaluate them.

Key
Excellent ✓✓✓✓ Very good ✓✓✓ Good ✓✓ Developing ✓

Information		Design	
Name		Menu presentation	
Type of food		Pictures	
Food and drinks		Colours	
Prices			

PLAN

6 Work in groups. Choose the theme for your food truck. Complete the steps below.

- Choose a name for your food truck.
- Decide on the design and illustrations for it.
- Decide and agree on the food you want to sell.
- Decide and agree on the prices.
- Plan and design the menu.
- Draw and illustrate your food truck.

PRESENT

7 Display your food truck design on your classroom wall. Remember to include an interesting menu with well organised information, an attractive design and the tips in *How to* evaluate a design.

CHECK

8 Look at your classmates' designs and complete the notes.

What is the theme of their food truck? ____________________

Which food truck has the best design? ____________________

Which food truck would you like to eat from? Why? ____________________

____

4 REVIEW

VOCABULARY

1 Complete the food words with the missing vowels.

1 w ___ t ___ r
2 ___ p p l ___
3 r ___ c ___
4 b ___ ___ n s
5 j ___ ___ c ___
6 c h ___ ___ s ___

2 Complete the sentences with the correct adjectives.

1 I've got a h________ lunch today: an egg, an apple and some water.
2 I hate beans. They taste d________ .
3 This burrito isn't very n________ . It's got onions in it and I don't like onions.
4 The tomatoes in this sandwich are f ________ . We get them from the garden every morning.
5 I love eating spiders. They're d________ .
6 Fizzy drinks have got a lot of sugar in them. They're u________ .

LANGUAGE IN ACTION

3 Are the words countable (C) or uncountable (U)?

1 beans ___
2 chocolate ___
3 worms ___
4 meat ___
5 rice ___
6 vegetable ___
7 tomato ___
8 milk ___

4 Complete the sentences. Use *a*, *an*, *some* or *any* and the correct food word.

1 Have you got ________ ________  ?
2 Sam always eats ________ ________  at break time.
3 Sorry. We haven't got ________ ________  .
4 I always have ________ ________  and ________ ________  for a snack.

5 Circle the correct words.

1 How *much* / *many* money have you got?
2 There *is* / *are* some rice and some chicken for dinner.
3 There's *much* / *a lot of* sugar in this drink. It's very unhealthy.
4 There *isn't* / *aren't* any carrots in the soup.
5 I don't eat *many* / *much* vegetables, but I eat *many* / *a lot of* fruit.
6 How *much* / *many* students *is* / *are* there in your class?
7 There *is* / *are* a lot of cheese in the fridge.
8 How *much* / *many* free time have you got at the weekend?
9 *Is there* / *Are there* any eggs? I want to make an omelette!
10 Why aren't there *much* / *many* books in the library?

Self-assessment

I can name fourteen food and drinks words in English.

I can use adjectives to describe food.

I can use countable and uncountable nouns with *a*/*an* and *some*/*any*.

I can use *there is*/*isn't* and *there are*/*aren't*.

LEARN TO ... PLAY VOCABULARY GAMES

Games can help you practise and remember new language.

1 Ask and answer with a partner.

1 What games do you like to play?
2 What is your favourite game?
3 Do you play any games to practise English?

OWN IT!

2 Work in pairs. Play Word Wizard.

1 Your partner chooses a letter of the alphabet. *a*

2 Write all the food or drink words you know beginning with the letter in 1 minute. Don't show your partner.
apples

3 Compare your lists. You get 5 points for a word on both lists. You get 10 points for a word on only your list.

4 Play the game again. This time you choose the letter of the alphabet.

5 The person with the most points is the **Word Wizard**.

3 Work in pairs. Play Three Clues.

Player A: Think of a food or drink. Don't say it! Give Player B three clues.

Player B: After each clue, guess Player A's word. Start with 3 points. Lose 1 point for each wrong guess.

Take turns to be **Player A** and **Player B**. The player with the most points at the end of the game is the winner.

Clue 1. They're healthy. — *Vegetables.*

No! Clue 2. They're sweet. — *Bananas!*

No. Last clue. Sometimes they're green and sometimes they're red. — *Apples!*

Yes, apples! You get 1 point!

4 Answer the questions. Write TC (Three Clues) or WW (Word Wizard).

1 Which game practises food nouns? ______
2 Which game practises food adjectives and food nouns? ______

5 Discuss with a partner. Think of word games you play in your language. Can you play them in English?

1 FINISHED?

1 Read the clues and write Esma's family members.

1 This is my mum's dad. *grandad*
2 This is my aunt and uncle's son. ______
3 This is my dad's brother. ______
4 This is my mum's mum. ______
5 This is my mum and dad's son. ______
6 This is my dad's sister. ______

2 Find and circle the things and family members Jack has got. Complete sentences 1–6.

sbsykmfootballsiscvkuncleauntnotboikanmcousinrtionhfugphonesjdeh

1 He *'s got* ______ a football.
2 He *hasn't got* ______ a sister.
3 He ______ an aunt.
4 He ______ a notebook.
5 He ______ a dictionary.
6 He ______ a phone.

FACT FILE

JENNIFER LAWRENCE
SISTERS 0
BROTHERS 2
EYES green
FRECKLES no
PET yes

3 Put the words in the correct order to make questions. Each question is in a different colour. Look at the fact file and answer the questions.

Has	got	she	and
she	green	got	sister
got	Has	eyes	got
she	sisters	a	has
freckles	she	Has	pet
twin	many	How	brothers
got	she	Has	a

1 *Has she got a twin sister?*
No, she hasn't got any sisters.
2 ______
3 ______
4 ______
5 ______

4 Read the descriptions and draw the people.

1
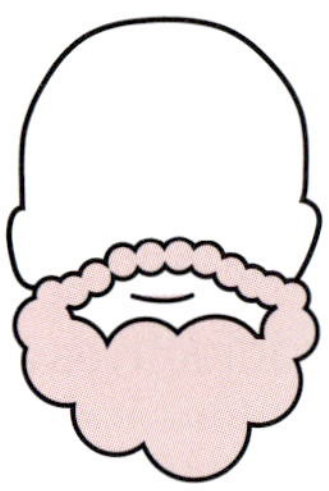
He's got a beard and a moustache, and long, red hair.

2

She's got short, wavy blonde hair and freckles.

3

She's got brown eyes, glasses and long, black hair.

2 FINISHED?

1 Look at the pictures and complete the sentences.

I  [1] *get up* ______ at 6.30 am and have my  [2] ______. Then I have a  [3] ______ and I get dressed. After that I  [4] ______ my teeth.

Before I leave the house, I pack my bag and quickly check my  [5] ______.

2 Put the letters in the correct order to make activities. Write what the people do at the weekend. Remember to use the correct form of the present simple.

1 y a l p t h i w d r i f e n s

Isabel *plays with friends.*

2 o d s i h w e m o r h o k

Matt ______

3 c t h a w T V

Mira and Fred ______

4 t o n o g o t c o o l s h

Ada ______

3 Circle words to make questions. Look at the pictures and answer the questions.

Yes, she does.

______

______

______

______

4 Read the clues and complete the crossword.

Across

1 I listen to this with my friends.

4 I love to read these.

5 I like to hang out with these people at the weekend.

6 I take these with my phone or camera.

Down

2 I play one of these to make music.

3 I play these games on my own.

3 FINISHED?

1 **Circle eight school subjects.**

A	M	A	V	O	P	Q	Q	M	J
Y	I	J	F	H	J	E	T	A	I
K	D	R	A	M	A	D	J	T	K
H	I	S	T	O	R	Y	S	H	L
O	I	C	D	R	T	L	M	S	M
U	G	I	H	G	Z	S	U	G	N
J	L	E	N	G	L	I	S	H	T
K	D	N	O	D	A	T	I	A	Y
H	Y	C	L	Y	J	A	C	L	H
F	G	E	O	G	R	A	P	H	Y

2 **Read the sentences and write the names.**

a 

Alex

b 

______

c 

______

d 

______

e 

______

1 Brian can sing and play the guitar.
2 Oscar can sing and play the piano.
3 Ryan can play the guitar but he can't sing.
4 Alex can sing very well but he can't play an instrument.
5 Guillermo can dance very well but he can't sing or play an instrument.

3 **Use the code to complete the sentences about Lara. Tick the ones that are true for you.**

A	C	D	E	G	H	I	K	L	M	N	O	P	S
✦	□	○	✪	💧	◗	🔔	■	☺	✸	☼	⌘	✈	❖

T	U	V	W
●	◆	🧲	◎

1 She ☺⌘🧲✪❖ ○✦☼□🔔☼💧
She loves dancing. ☐
2 She ◗✦●✪❖ 💧✪●●🔔☼💧 ◆✈
She ______ ☐
3 She ○⌘✪❖☼'● ✸🔔☼○ ◎✦☺■🔔☼💧
She ______ ☐
4 She ○⌘✪❖☼'● ☺🔔■✪ □⌘⌘■🔔☼💧
She ______ ☐
5 She ☺🔔■✪❖ ❖◎🔔✸✸🔔☼💧
She ______ ☐

4 **Where are they? Look at the photos and write the correct place.**

1 
2 
3 
4 
5 

1 Antoni is in the canteen.
2 Alicia is on the ______.
3 Mehmet is in the ______.
4 Max and Irina are in the ______.
5 Mr White and Miss Green are in the ______.

4 FINISHED?

1 **Complete the table with the words in the box. Circle the foods you like to eat.**

apples bananas beans chicken chocolate fish fizzy drink juice meat rice water

Lunch or dinner	Drink	Snack
		apples

2 **Circle the four countable foods and underline the four uncountable foods.**

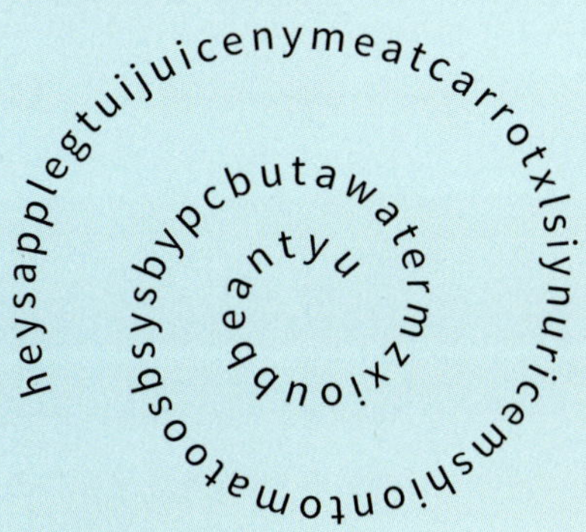

3 **Put the letters in the correct order to make a word. Write a sentence about the photo.**

1 lapsep *There aren't any apples.*
2 nabaan
3 gegs
4 trocars
5 blatesegev

4 **Match photos a–f with descriptions 1–6.**

a  *4*

b 

c 

d 

e 

f 

1 This is cold, fresh and healthy but not sweet.
2 These are cold, fresh, healthy and sweet.
3 These are hot and healthy.
4 This is cold, sweet and unhealthy.
5 These are salty and unhealthy but not hot.
6 This is hot and unhealthy.

STARTER VOCABULARY BANK

Months

January	May	September
February	June	October
March	July	November
April	August	December

Colours

blue	purple
green	red
orange	yellow
pink	white

1 Ask five students in your class to tell you the date of their birthdays.

When is your birthday?

My birthday is on the fifteenth of August.

Classroom objects

board

calculator

chair

dictionary

door

notebook

pen

pencil

poster

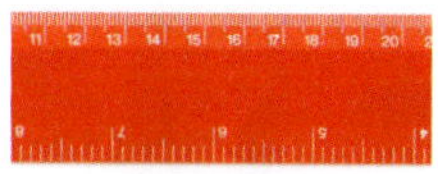
ruler

table

window

2 Find six classroom objects. Can you see these objects in your classroom? What colour are they? Write sentences.

1 *My dictionary is red and blue.*
2 ______
3 ______
4 ______
5 ______
6 ______

D	I	C	T	I	O	N	A	R	Y
F	E	A	N	I	T	O	M	P	E
W	I	L	L	B	E	T	N	O	R
H	J	C	A	S	P	E	N	T	C
A	R	U	B	E	V	B	I	R	U
R	U	L	E	R	T	O	V	E	R
C	H	A	R	T	X	O	R	L	E
I	C	T	O	R	E	K	L	O	P
G	I	O	N	E	R	A	U	H	I
T	R	R	P	P	E	N	C	I	L

LEARN TO LEARN

Using your own language

When you learn a new word in English, write a translation in your own language to help you to remember it.

3 Write a list of the classroom objects in Exercise 2. Write translations in your own language. Cover the English words. Can you remember them?

1 ______ ______
2 ______ ______
3 ______ ______
4 ______ ______
5 ______ ______
6 ______ ______

1 VOCABULARY BANK

Friends and family

aunt	grandad	mum	uncle
brother	granddaughter	nephew	wife
cousin	grandma	niece	
dad	grandson	sister	
daughter	husband	son	

1 Write true/false sentences about the people in your family. Tell your partner. Can they guess which sentences are false?

1 *My grandma is 100 years old.*
2 ______
3 ______
4 ______
5 ______

Describing people

beard

blonde

brown

freckles

glasses

grey

long

moustache

red

short

tall

wavy

2 Circle the correct words.

1 My baby sister has got *a beard* / *freckles* / *a moustache*.
2 My grandad is *tall* / *wavy* / *long*.
3 My cousin's eyes are *short* / *red* / *brown*.
4 My grandma has got *glasses* / *grey* / *blonde*.

LEARN TO LEARN

Drawing pictures

Drawing pictures can help you to remember new words.

3 Use the words for describing people to describe someone in your family to your partner. Ask your partner to draw the person. Does it look like them?

My brother is tall and has short brown hair and glasses.

2 VOCABULARY BANK

Daily routines

brush your teeth

check your phone

do your homework

get dressed

get up

go home

go to bed

go to school

have a shower

have breakfast

pack your bag

wake up

1 Match 1–4 with a–d to make sentences.

1 I usually have
2 I pack
3 On school mornings I wake
4 I go to

a my school bag in the evening.
b a shower in the morning.
c school on the bus.
d up at six o'clock.

Leisure activities

chat online	go shopping	make videos	read a book/magazine
download songs	hang out with friends	play an instrument	take photos
go for a bike ride	listen to music	play video games	watch TV

2 Put the letters in order to complete the sentences.

1 My brother *eswtcha VT* __________ __________ before he goes to bed.
2 I *og goppshin* __________ __________ with my friends.
3 He *ckches* __________ his *nepho* __________ all the time.
4 He *sketa osotph* __________ __________ with his new camera.

LEARN TO LEARN

Word partners

When you learn new words, learn words that go with them to improve your vocabulary.

3 Make six word partners from the words in the box.

a bike ride | read | music | your homework | dressed | watch | listen to | go for | do | TV | a magazine | get

1 ______________________
2 ______________________
3 ______________________
4 ______________________
5 ______________________
6 ______________________

3 VOCABULARY BANK

School subjects

art
design and technology (DT)
drama
English
food technology
geography
history
information and communication technology (ICT)
maths
music
physical education (PE)
science
Spanish

1 Circle the correct words.

1 We learn about mountains and rivers in *geography / history*.
2 We draw pictures in *English / art*.
3 We have fun being actors in *drama / science*.
4 In *maths / music* we learn about numbers.
5 We speak another language in *Spanish / maths*.

Places in a school

canteen

classroom

ICT room

library

locker area

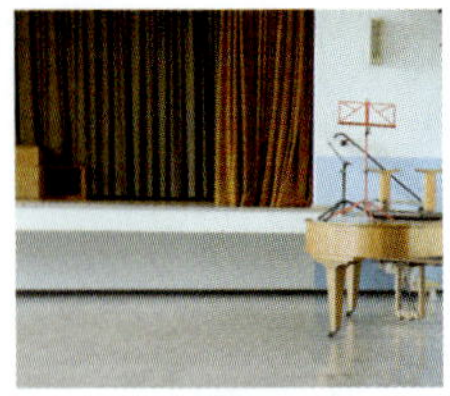
main hall

playing field

reception

science lab

sports hall

staffroom

toilets

2 Find and circle six places in a school.

luartllibraryhotpowreceptionaumusicstaffroomqoiseatoiletsbscienceolockerroomcadramaosportshallasi

LEARN TO LEARN

Making a spidergram

You can use spidergrams to help learn new vocabulary. They show you how words are related.

3 Which words in the box can you use in a spidergram about each place? Write the words next to the places 1–4.

outside	computer	food	program	mouse	online	history
board	meal	PE	desk	maths	lunch	running	eat	football

1 canteen: __________
2 playing field: __________
3 classroom: __________
4 ICT room: __________

4 VOCABULARY BANK

Food and drink

apples

bananas

beans

carrots

cheese

chicken

chocolate

eggs

fish

fizzy drink

juice

meat

rice

water

1 **Look at the pictures. How often do you eat or drink these? Compare your answers with your partner.**

every day: ______________________ sometimes: ______________________

often: ______________________ never: ______________________

Adjectives

cold	disgusting	healthy	nice	sweet
delicious	fresh	hot	salty	unhealthy

2 **Match the words in the box with the meanings 1–5.**

sweet healthy delicious disgusting unhealthy

1 This word describes a food you hate. __________

2 This word describes a food you love. __________

3 This food isn't good for you. __________

4 This word describes food with a lot of sugar in it. __________

5 This food is good for you. __________

LEARN TO LEARN

True or false sentences

Correcting false statements helps you to remember information.

3 **Use the adjectives above to write true and false sentences. Say your sentences. Your partner says if they are true or false and corrects the false sentences.**

1 ______________________________

2 ______________________________

3 ______________________________

4 ______________________________

5 ______________________________

Crisps are sweet.

False. They are salty.

2 MATHS

1 When do you use maths in your daily activities?

2.14 2 Read the article. Are any of your ideas from Exercise 1 in the article?

3 Match the words in **bold** in the text with the examples.

1 ______________ : 1 kg, two cups
2 ______________ : $\frac{7}{8}$, $\frac{4}{5}$
3 ______________ : 45%, 99%

4 Read the article again and look at the pictures. Answer the questions in blue.

1 ______________
2 ______________
3 ______________

5 Are the sentences *T* (true) or *F* (false)?

1 We don't need fractions in real life. ___
2 We use maths every time we tell the time. ___
3 'A quarter' and 'half' are examples of percentages. ___

Explore it!

Do the calculation.

Write the number of the month you were born. Multiply by 4. Add 13. Multiply by 25. Subtract 200. Add the day of the month you were born. Multiply by 2. Subtract 40. Multiply by 50. Add the last two numbers of the year you were born. Subtract 10,500.

- The first two numbers are the month you were born.
- The next two numbers are the day you were born.
- The last two numbers are the year you were born.

Find an interesting maths puzzle and test your partner.

Everyday maths

Your maths teacher gives you homework on fractions. 'I don't need **fractions** in real life,' you think. 'What's the point?' In fact, maths is everywhere.

Telling the time

'Excuse me, what time is it?' someone asks. You look at your phone. 'It's a quarter to four,' you reply. This is a really mathematical sentence, and you need to know about fractions! [1]How many minutes are there in the fractions 'a quarter', 'half' and 'three-quarters'?

Shopping

You want some new clothes, so you go shopping. You see something nice and a sign says there is 40% off the original price of £20. Then you see another offer … 50% off the original price of £26. [2]Which item is cheaper? It helps to know how **percentages** work before you waste money!

Cooking

You want to make your favourite biscuits. The recipe asks for two tablespoons of sugar, but you only have a teaspoon. [3]How many teaspoons make two tablespoons? You may know the answer, but that's because you understand maths and **measurements**!

We use maths every day of our lives. So, the next time your maths teacher gives you homework, make sure you do it!

4 ART

1 **Look carefully at the photo. What can you see?**

4.12 2 **Read the article. Write what the food represents in the photo.**

1 broccoli ________

2 fruit ________

3 **Are the sentences *T* (true) or *F* (false)?**

1 We need to look at the photo again to understand it. ___

2 The photo shows a dream. ___

3 Warner makes the photos with other people. ___

4 He doesn't eat all the food at the end of the session. ___

4 **Check the meaning of the words in yellow in the article.**

Explore it!

Guess the correct answer.

Carl Warner also makes food photos of famous buildings. What is the main ingredient in his photo of the Taj Mahal?

a chicken b onions c bread

Find an interesting fact about food and art. Write a question for your partner to answer.

Foodscapes

There are many works of art about food. But there are also times when art is food. Literally.

Look at the photo. What can you see? There are some houses and trees and there are a lot of balloons in the sky. It is a beautiful **landscape**!

Now look again. Those aren't trees ... they are pieces of broccoli! And those balloons are all different types of fruit!

Don't worry, you are not dreaming. Photographer Carl Warner loves making landscapes out of food because he loves their connection with the natural world. He calls them 'foodscapes' and the results are amazing.

Warner takes three days to prepare a photograph. First, he decides which ingredients to use. Then he builds the **scene** with his team. Next, he takes photos in **layers**. There is a lot of fresh food, so he works quickly under the hot lights. What happens to the food at the end of a session? He shares it with his team, of course!

First, Warner wants to make people smile. However, he also wants to **promote** a good diet. With these **surreal** images, he makes us think about food in a different way.

PRONUNCIATION

UNIT 1

/h/

1.07 **1 Listen and repeat.**

/h/ have got Hey! home husband

1.08 **2 Listen and circle the option you hear.**

1 (hat) / at
2 hair / air
3 has / as
4 hand / and

1.09 **3 Listen and repeat the sentences.**

1 Hunter has got brown hair and he is happy.
2 Hey! How are things?

4 Practise saying the sentences in Exercise 3.

UNIT 2

/s/, /z/ and /ɪz/

2.05 **1 Listen and repeat.**

/s/ speak**s** /z/ doe**s** /ɪz/ chang**es**

2.06 **2 Listen and write A (/s/ or /z/) or B (/ɪz/).**

1 goes A
2 studies ___
3 eats ___
4 teaches ___

3 Add *-s* or *-es* to the verbs and put them in the correct column.

break___ catch___ choose___ go___ read___ think___ watch___

/s/ **or** /z/	/ɪz/
breaks	

2.07 **4 Listen, check and repeat.**

5 Cover the table in Exercise 3 and take turns to say a verb from the box. Your partner says the verb with the *-s* ending.

UNIT 3

can

3.03 **1 Listen and repeat.**

1 /kən/ She can play the piano.
2 /kən/ Can he read music?
3 /kæn/ Yes, he can.
4 /kɑːnt/ She can't go.

3.04 **2 Listen and circle the option you hear.**

1 I (*can*) / *can't* hear you.
2 Pablo *can* / *can't* help you with your homework.
3 They *can* / *can't* count to 20 in Russian.
4 *Can* / *Can't* you use your phone at school?

3 Read the conversation. Write the numbers (1–7) in the correct column.

/kən/	/kæn/	/kɑːnt/
1		

BETH Hi, Tim. [1]Can I ask you some questions?
TIM Yes, you [2]can. Of course.
BETH Great. [3]Can you swim?
TIM No, I [4]can't.
BETH [5]Can you draw or paint?
TIM Yes, I [6]can.
BETH And [7]can you speak Spanish?
TIM *Sí*! I mean yes.

3.05 **4 Listen and check. Practise the conversation.**

UNIT 4

Word stress

1 How many syllables have these words got?

apples [2] vegetable [ ] disgusting [ ] unhealthy [ ] salty [ ] water [ ]

4.06 **2 Listen and check.**

3 Match the words in Exercise 1 with the stress patterns (1–3).

1 Oo apples
2 oOo ___
3 Ooo ___

4.07 **4 Listen, check and repeat.**

OWN IT! 1

A2 Key test content in *Own It!* Level 1 has been checked by Cambridge Assessment English for accuracy and level.

WORKBOOK

Vicki Anderson and Lynn Durrant

CAMBRIDGE
UNIVERSITY PRESS

CONTENTS

STARTER
WELCOME!

VOCABULARY AND READING

Months, cardinal and ordinal numbers and colours

1 ☆ **Complete the sentences with the months in the box and ordinal numbers.**

April	August	February	~~January~~
June	March	November	October

1 *January* is the first month.
2 ________ is the ________ month.
3 ________ is the third month.
4 ________ is the ________ month.
5 May is the ________ month.
6 ________ is the sixth month.
7 July is the ________ month.
8 ________ is the ________ month.
9 September is the ________ month.
10 ________ is the tenth month.
11 ________ is the ________ month.
12 December is the ________ month.

2 ☆☆ **Complete the crossword. Write seven more colours.**

ACROSS →
2 three letters
3 four letters
4 six letters
7 five letters
8 five letters

DOWN ↓
1 five letters
5 six letters
6 four letters

Online profile

3 ☆☆ **Read about Dasha and Carlos. Where are their friends from?**

Home | **Profile** | Photos | Events

INTERNATIONAL STUDENT PROFILE DAY!

Hello! My name's Dasha. I'm from Warsaw in Poland. I'm 11. How old are you? In this photo, I'm with my two best friends. Polina is Polish, but Marta isn't Polish. She's Brazilian. My favourite colour is green. What's your favourite colour? My birthday is on 10th April. When's your birthday? My dream is to be a doctor! What's your dream? Write soon!

Hi, Dasha! I'm Carlos and I'm 11, too! I'm Mexican, from Mexico City. In this photo, I'm with my best friends. They're not Mexican. Yusuf is from Turkey and David is from England. My favourite colour is blue. I'm 12 tomorrow! It's 5th June and it's my birthday! My dream is to be a singer! Who's your favourite singer? Let me know! ☺

4 **Read the profiles again and complete the table.**

Name	Birthday	Favourite colour	Dream
Dasha	10th April	green	4 ________
1 *Carlos*	2 ________	3 ________	singer

5 ☆☆ **Circle the correct answers.**

1 Dasha is from *China* / *(Poland)*.
2 Her birthday is in the *fourth* / *seventh* month of the year.
3 Carlos is from *Turkey* / *Mexico*.
4 His birthday is in the *sixth* / *twelfth* month of the year.
5 *David* / *Carlos* is 12 tomorrow.

LANGUAGE IN ACTION AND VOCABULARY

Subject pronouns and possessive adjectives

1 ☆ **Complete the table with the subject pronouns in the box.**

it they we ~~you~~

Singular	Plural
I	3 ______
1 ___you___	you
he / she / 2 ______	4 ______

2 ☆ **Write the subject pronoun.**

1 Dasha ___she___
2 photos ______
3 school ______
4 Carlos ______
5 Polina and Marta ______
6 Yusuf and I ______

3 ☆ **Which plural pronoun can we use for objects and people?**

______

4 ☆ **Complete the sentences with the possessive adjectives in the box.**

her his its my our ~~their~~ your

1 Yusuf and Carlos are at school. They're in ___their___ classroom.
2 He's from Poland. ______ name's Max.
3 I'm 12 years old and ______ best friend, Alba, is 11.
4 We're from China. ______ nationality is Chinese.
5 You're 13. ______ birthday is in April.
6 My teacher is Maria. ______ birthday is in August.
7 This school is nice. ______ classrooms are big!

Verb *be*

5 ☆☆ **Complete the profile with the correct form of *be*.**

My name [1] ___is___ Sofía. I [2] ______ from Chile. My best friend [3] ______ Ana. She [4] ______ (not) from Chile. She [5] ______ from Brazil. My favourite singer [6] ______ Lorde. My favourite songs [7] ______ *Green Light* and *Royals*. They [8] ______ brilliant!

Question words

6 ☆ **Match questions 1–5 with answers a–e.**

1 Where are you from? [c]
2 How old are you? [ ]
3 When's your birthday? [ ]
4 Who's your best friend? [ ]
5 What's your favourite number? [ ]

a 10th May.
b It's 15.
c ~~I'm from Paris.~~
d That's Alba.
e I'm 11.

Classroom objects

7 ☆ **Look at the pictures. Circle the correct words.**

1 It's a *board* / *(calculator)*.
2 They're *chairs* / *desks*.
3 It's a *window* / *door*.
4 They're *pens* / *pencils*.
5 It's a *pen* / *pencil*.
6 They're *rulers* / *notebooks*.

LISTENING AND LANGUAGE IN ACTION

A talk

1 ☆ **Listen and circle the correct answer.** (S.01)

Elena's from *Spain / Brazil*.

2 ☆ **Listen again. Number the instructions in the order you hear them (1–4).** (S.01)

a

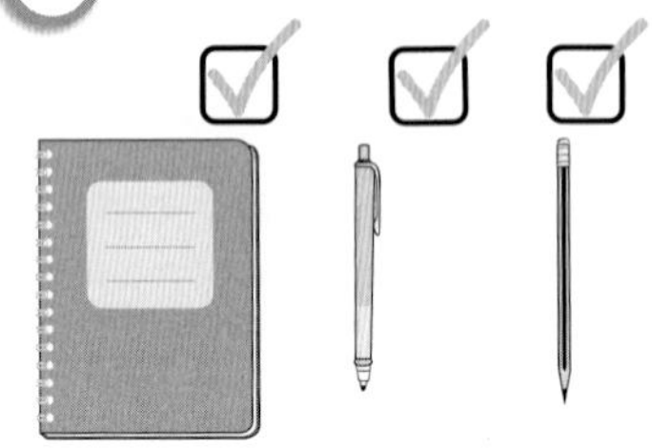

b

☐ ☐

c

d

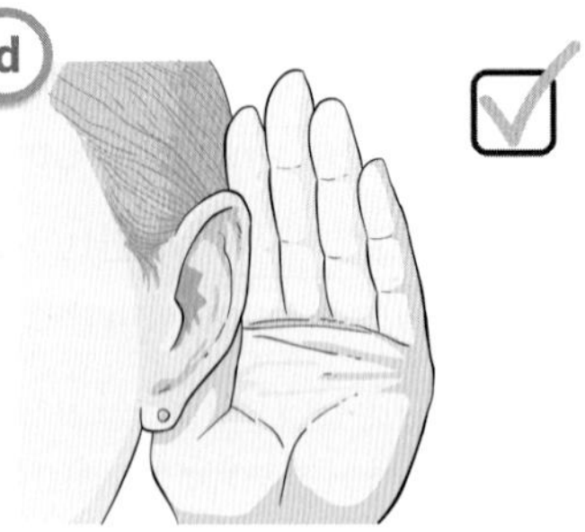

[1] ☐

3 ☆☆ **Listen again. Are the sentences *T* (true) or *F* (false)?** (S.01)

1 This is Elena's first day at school. ___T___
2 She's from the capital of Brazil. ______
3 She's the only student from Brazil in her class. ______
4 Her notebook is on her desk. ______
5 Her pens and pencils are in her schoolbag. ______
6 The ruler on the desk is hers. ______

Whose + possessive pronouns

4 ☆☆ **Complete the sentences with the correct possessive pronouns.**

1 Whose dictionaries are these?
They're their dictionaries. They're ___theirs___ .
2 Whose ruler is this?
It's my ruler. It's ______ .
3 Whose books are these?
They're our books. They're ______ .
4 Whose poster is that?
It's her poster. It's ______ .
5 Whose chairs are those? They're your chairs.
They're ______ .
6 Whose calculator is this? It's his calculator.
It's ______ .

Imperatives

5 ☆☆ **Put the words in the correct order to make sentences.**

1 write / Don't / notebook / my / in
Don't write in my notebook.
2 board / the / Write / the / words / on
______
3 late / Don't / for / be / class
______
4 teacher / to / Listen / the
______
5 eat / in / class / Don't
______
6 book / your / Close
______

6 ☆☆☆ **Write two more instructions for your class.**

______
______
______
______

WRITING

An informal letter

1 ☆ **Read Jenny's letter. Who is from Australia?**

____

20 Marsh Street
York
Yorkshire
DN14 68YK

20th October

Dear Lucy,

1 My name is Jenny Watts and I'm 12. I'm from York in England.

2 My school is great. The classroom is green, orange and white. It's very nice, with lots of posters on the walls. Our teacher is friendly and I'm happy in my new class.

3 My best friend isn't in my class. She's at a different school. She isn't English like me, she's Australian. Her name is Sarah.

4 My favourite object is my new red and blue notebook. My favourite number is five – my birthday is 5th May! My dream is to be a famous singer.

All the best,

Jenny

2 ☆ **Read the letter again. Match topics a–d with paragraphs 1–4.**

a favourite object, number, birthday and dream ☐

b name, age and nationality [1]

c best friend ☐

d school and class ☐

3 ☆ **Match phrases 1–3 with functions a–c.**

1 All the best, ☐

2 Our teacher is friendly <u>and</u> I'm happy in my new class. ☐

3 Dear Lucy, ☐

a to start a letter

b to end a letter

c to join two ideas in one sentence

Write an informal letter.

PLAN

4 ☆☆ **Decide what information to include in each paragraph. Use the information in Exercise 2 to help you.**

WRITE

5 ☆☆☆ **Write your letter. Remember to include four paragraphs, the address and date, and expressions from the *Useful language* box (see Student's Book, p9).**

CHECK

6 **Do you …**

- introduce yourself and give your name, age and nationality?
- use *and* to join ideas?
- say what your dream is?

1 FRIENDS AND FAMILY

VOCABULARY

Family members

1 ☆ **Find 13 more words for family in the word search.**

W	G	N	E	P	H	E	W	G	S	O	N
B	R	O	T	H	E	R	D	F	T	S	E
R	A	D	G	U	J	I	N	K	M	O	X
A	N	U	T	S	S	K	J	I	E	A	Y
V	D	W	H	B	C	U	N	C	L	E	D
G	M	U	M	A	K	E	H	K	M	Y	A
D	A	T	S	N	H	D	A	D	W	D	U
G	R	A	N	D	A	D	E	Q	I	F	G
R	G	U	W	J	O	P	R	T	F	Q	H
B	D	N	I	E	C	E	I	M	E	P	T
F	G	T	K	H	O	S	N	G	X	V	E
C	O	U	S	I	N	S	I	S	T	E	R

2 ☆ **Match 1–8 with a–h to make family word pairs.**

1 brother [f] a mum
2 nephew [ ] b wife
3 husband [ ] c daughter
4 grandad [ ] d aunt
5 uncle [ ] e grandma
6 dad [ ] f ~~sister~~
7 son [ ] g granddaughter
8 grandson [ ] h niece

3 ☆ **Which family word in Exercise 1 can be male or female?** ______

4 ☆☆ **Look at Ana's family tree. Complete her sentences with the correct family words.**

1 Carlos is my *grandad* and María is my ______.
2 Marta is my ______ and David is my ______.
3 Javier is my ______ and Lucía is my ______.
4 Lucas is my ______.
5 Pedro and Julia are my ______.

5 ☆☆ **Circle the correct answer.**

DAVID Hi! I'm David and my sisters are April, May and June. This is my mum.

MUM Hi! I'm a mum with four children. My daughters are April, May and June and this is my son. His name is ______.

a July b September c David

Explore it!

Guess the correct answer.

______ is the most popular boy's name in the UK in the last 500 years.

a Robert b John c James

Find another interesting fact about names. Then send a question in an email to a classmate or ask them it in the next class.

READING

A webpage

1 Read the webpage. What is it about? Circle the correct title.

a A big family

b A small family

c A family from Canada

2 Read the webpage again and underline the words. Then check their meaning and complete the sentences.

dentist	everyone	fun	~~neighbours~~	whole

1 Your house is next to mine. We're neighbours .

2 My aunt is a ______________ . Her job is to look at teeth!

3 A ______________ day is 24 hours long.

4 My favourite day is Sunday with friends and family. It's ______________ !

5 This lesson is for all students. It's for ______________ .

3 Read the webpage again. Are the sentences *T* (true) or *F* (false)?

1 Tom is English. T

2 His mum is a teacher. ______

3 His family is typical because it's big. ______

4 His cousins are in a different street. ______

5 The family are together in the morning and evening. ______

6 Tom is happy at home. ______

4 Circle the options that are true for you.

1 My family is *big / small*.

2 My favourite time of day is the *morning / evening*.

3 My neighbours *are / aren't* at my birthday parties.

Tom is from Durham in England. He's seven years old today! His parents' names are Helen and Richard. His mum is a dentist and his dad is a teacher at a secondary school.

Tom's family isn't very typical. He's got two brothers and three sisters, and his grandma and grandad are at home with them, too. Tom's aunt, uncle and four cousins have got a house in front of his. The whole family are in the same street!

Tom's favourite times are the morning and the evening. That's when his family are all together for breakfast and dinner – there are ten people around the table!

Birthdays in Tom's family are fun, too. They've got a birthday party every month! Today, everyone is at Tom's party: his family, his friends and his neighbours.

Is Tom happy in his big family? Yes, he's got good friends at school, and lots of brothers, sisters and cousins at home!

LANGUAGE IN ACTION

have got: affirmative and negative

1 ☆ Circle the correct options.

1 Richard and Helen (*have*) / *has* got six children.
2 My grandma *have* / *has* got a red car.
3 I *haven't* / *hasn't* got a big family.
4 My dad *haven't* / *hasn't* got any cousins.
5 My friend's parents *have* / *has* got a big house.
6 Uncle David *haven't* / *hasn't* got any children.

2 ☆☆ Complete the text with the correct form of *have got*.

My name is Claudia. I'm from Mexico but I live in Australia with my family. I [1] *'ve got* a big family. I [2] ______ five brothers and two sisters. My parents [3] ______ a big house – it's perfect for a big family! My dad's name is Javier. He [4] ______ lots of brothers and sisters, too. My mum is called Sandra. She [5] ______ a brother in Mexico – that's my Uncle Sergio. I [6] ______ any aunts or uncles in Australia. They're all in different countries. My best friend, Helen, is Australian. She [7] ______ any brothers or sisters, it's only her! She [8] ______ a small family, but they're good fun! 🙂

3 ☆☆ Write the words in the correct order to make sentences. Then match them with pictures a–e.

1 bike / I / haven't / a / got
I haven't got a bike. [b]
2 My / got / grandad / hasn't / a / mobile phone
______ [ ]
3 home! / We've / pets / at / four / got
______ [ ]
4 best friends / at / school / two / I've / got
______ [ ]
5 My / two / got / boards / classroom's
______ [ ]

Possessive *'s*

4 ☆☆ Complete the sentences with the possessive *'s* and a family word.

1 My mum *'s mum* is my grandma.
2 My cousin ______ is my uncle.
3 My dad ______ is my uncle.
4 My mum ______ is my aunt.
5 My brother ______ is my mum.
6 My dad ______ is my grandad.

5 ☆☆☆ Find four facts about a famous family. Write four sentences about them. Use the correct form of *have got* and the possessive *'s*.

Victoria and David Beckham have got four children.

______

______

______

______

VOCABULARY AND LISTENING

Describing people

1 ★ **Complete the list with the words in the box.**

blonde freckles ~~grey~~ tall wavy

Describing people

Eyes: [1] *grey*, brown

Hairstyle: long, short, [2] ________

Hair colour: [3] ________, brown, grey, red

Height: [4] ________, short

Other features: beard, [5] ________, glasses, moustache

2 ★ **Match the descriptions (1–4) with the photos (a–d).**

1 glasses and long wavy hair
2 long hair and a beard
3 long blonde hair
4 short brown hair and glasses

a

b

c

d

A conversation

1.01 **3** ★★ **Listen to the students talking about their families. Write *Paul's family*, *Emma's family*, *Jon's family* or *Sue's family* under the correct pictures.**

1

____

2

____

3

____

4

____

1.01 **4** ★★ **Listen again. Circle the correct answers.**

1 Paul's got (*four*) / *five* brothers and sisters.
2 Paul *has* / *hasn't* got blonde hair.
3 Emma's sister *has* / *hasn't* got freckles.
4 Emma's got a friend with *long* / *short* hair.
5 Jon's got *one brother* / *two brothers*.
6 Jon's mum *is* / *isn't* short.
7 Sue's got *one tall brother* / *two tall brothers*.
8 *Sue's* / *Tony's* hair is red.

5 ★★★ **Describe a friend. Include information from each category in Exercise 1.**

My friend's name is Cindy. She's got brown eyes and long red hair.

____

LANGUAGE IN ACTION

have got: questions

1 ★ **Complete the table with *have*, *has*, *hasn't* or *haven't*.**

[1] Have you got any cousins?	Yes, I [2] ______.	No, I [3] ______.
[4] ______ they got red hair?	Yes, they [5] ______.	No, they [6] ______.
[7] ______ she got green eyes?	Yes, she [8] ______.	No, she [9] ______.
How many sisters [10] ______ he got?	He [11] ______ got two sisters.	

2 ★ **Complete the questions with the correct form of *have got*. Then match them with answers a–f.**

1 Have you got any brothers and sisters? [b]
2 ______ your niece ______ brown hair? [ ]
3 ______ you and your family ______ a big house? [ ]
4 ______ your dad ______ a beard? [ ]
5 ______ your parents ______ a car? [ ]
6 ______ your house ______ a lot of rooms? [ ]

a No, he hasn't.
b ~~No, I haven't.~~
c Yes, they have.
d Yes, she has.
e Yes, it has.
f No, we haven't.

3 ★★ **Complete the conversation with the correct form of *have got* and the words in brackets.**

BETH Hi, Jan. [1] Have you got (you) a lot of homework?
JAN No, I [2] ______.
BETH Good. I've got some questions for a school project. [3] ______ (you) any brothers and sisters?
JAN Yes, I [4] ______. I've got two brothers. They're twins.
BETH [5] ______ (they) green eyes like you?
JAN Yes, they [6] ______!
BETH Cool! And [7] ______ (your mum) brown hair like you?
JAN No, she [8] ______. She's got blonde hair.

4 ★★★ **Read the answers from an interview with a famous actor. Write questions with *have got*. Use *how many* when necessary.**

1 Have you got a big house?
Yes, I have. My house is very big.
2 ______?
Yes, we've got five children, including twins!
3 ______?
We've got three boys and two girls.
4 ______?
My wife's got a horse, and the children have got two rabbits.
5 ______?
Yes, I have. I've got two Oscars!

WRITING

An informal email

1 ★ Look at the photos and read the email. Which photo is of Kylie and Kate? Tick (✓) the correct photo.

a

b

TO: Ed

FROM: Kate

Hi Ed,

1 How are things? I'm in a new school and I've got a new friend. This email is about her.

2 I [1]*'m* / *'ve* got a lot of friends in my class, but one girl [2]*'s* / *'ve* my best friend. Her name [3]*'re* / *'s* Kylie. We say we [4]*'re* / *'ve* twins – we look the same! We [5]*'s* / *'ve* got brown hair and green eyes, and we [6]*'re* / *'ve* got the same birthday! It [7]*'s* / *'re* funny! And we [8]*'s* / *'ve* both got a little brother. My brother [9]*'re* / *'s* ten and Kylie's brother [10]*'s* / *'re* nine.

3 The photo is of Kylie and me at basketball. Kylie's good fun and a great friend.

4 Have you got good friends at your new school? Have you got a best friend? Email me soon!

That's all for now,

Kate

2 ★★ Circle the correct contractions in the email.

3 ★★ Read the email again. Are the sentences *T* (true) or *F* (false)?

1 Kate and Kylie are best friends. T
2 They are in different classes. ____
3 Their birthdays are on the same day. ____
4 Kate hasn't got brown hair. ____
5 Kylie hasn't got green eyes. ____
6 They have both got a little brother. ____
7 Kate's brother is ten. ____

4 ★★ Match topics a–d with paragraphs 1–4 in the email.

a extra information about a photo [3]
b description of a new friend at school [ ]
c introduction and reason for writing [ ]
d Kate's questions for Ed [ ]

Write an informal email to a friend about a new school friend.

PLAN

5 ★★ Make notes about these things:

your friend's name and age

______

your friend's physical description and family

______

6 Decide what information to include in each paragraph. Use the information in Exercise 4 to help you.

WRITE

7 ★★★ Remember to include four paragraphs, the verbs *be* and *have got* and expressions from the *Useful language* box (see Student's Book, p17).

CHECK

8 Do you ...

- use expressions to start and end your email?
- give information about your friend in the second paragraph?
- use information from a photo in the third paragraph?
- ask questions in the last paragraph?

1 REVIEW

VOCABULARY

1 Look at the family tree. Are the sentences *T* (true) or *F* (false)? Correct the false sentences.

1 Ashley is Kyle's cousin.

2 Jane is Mary's daughter.

3 Jon is Ashley's grandad.

4 Luke is Andrea's cousin.

5 Jane is Kyle's mum.

6 Luke is Jane's brother.

7 Kyle and Harry are Jon's grandsons.

8 Ashley is Rob's aunt.

9 Rob is Ashley and Kyle's dad.

10 Holly and Ashley are Mary's nieces.

2 Circle the odd one out.

1 moustache / beard / tall
2 wavy / glasses / short
3 blonde / freckles / brown
4 blue / green / short
5 long / blonde / red
6 brown / tall / wavy

LANGUAGE IN ACTION

3 Circle the correct options.

Victor and Anna [1]*has* / *have* got a big house. It [2]*'s* / *'ve* got a big garden and seven rooms. They [3]*'s* / *'ve* got one daughter called Siena. They [4]*haven't* / *have* got any sons. Anna and Siena [5]*has* / *have* got blonde hair. Anna [6]*'s* / *'ve* got blue eyes, and Siena [7]*'s* / *'ve* got brown eyes. Victor [8]*'s* / *'ve* got three sports cars. They're his favourite! Anna [9]*hasn't* / *haven't* got a sports car, but she [10]*'s* / *'ve* got a mobile home!

4 **Write questions with the correct form of *have got*. Use *how many* when necessary. Then look at Exercise 3 and answer the questions.**

1 Victor and Anna / a big garden?

_______________ _______________

2 rooms / their house?

_______________ _______________

3 they / sons?

_______________ _______________

4 Siena / blonde hair?

_______________ _______________

5 sports cars / Victor?

_______________ _______________

6 Anna / mobile home?

_______________ _______________

CUMULATIVE LANGUAGE

5 **Match questions 1–8 with answers a–h.**

1 Have your grandparents got a big garden? ☐
2 What have we got for homework? ☐
3 How many cousins have you got? ☐
4 Have you got an English dictionary? ☐
5 Has your dad got a beard? ☐
6 When have we got our exam? ☐
7 Is that Amalia's baby brother? ☐
8 Wow! How many books have your parents got? ☐

a I've got four.
b Yes, they have. It's my favourite place!
c I don't know. I think they've got hundreds!
d No, he hasn't! But he's got a moustache.
e Yes, I have.
f We've got the exercises on page 14.
g No! It's her nephew. He's her sister's baby.
h I'm not sure. I think it's in November.

2 THAT'S LIFE!

VOCABULARY

Daily routines

1 ☆ **Complete the crossword. Use the clues.**

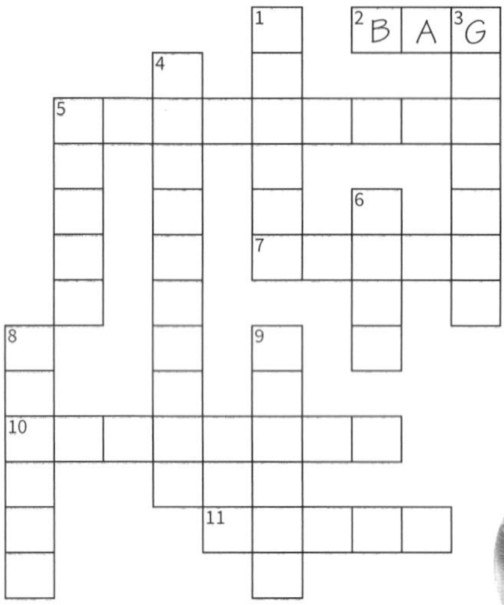

ACROSS

2 You pack your ___bag___ with your books for school.

5 I have ___________ with my family. We have cereal.

7 After school, you check your ___________ for messages.

10 At secondary school, you do your ___________ every evening.

11 First you wake up. Then you ___________.

DOWN

1 I ___________ at seven o'clock, but I get up at 7.15.

3 At night, you ___________ and sleep.

4 In the morning, I ___________ in my school uniform.

5 I ___________ my teeth after breakfast and before I go to bed.

6 After school, I go ___________ on the bus.

8 I go to ___________ from Monday to Friday, but not at the weekend!

9 I have a ___________ when I get up and after sport.

2 ☆ **Complete the daily routines with the verbs in the box.**

brush check do get (x2) go (x3) have (x2) pack wake

1 ___get___ up		7 ______ to school	
2 ______ dressed		8 ______ my phone	
3 ______ my teeth		9 ______ to bed	
4 ______ breakfast		10 ______ up	
5 ______ home		11 ______ a shower	
6 ______ my bag		12 ______ my homework	

3 ☆☆ **Complete the text with the correct form of the phrases from Exercise 2.**

This is my ideal school day. I [1] ___wake up___ at nine o'clock and I [2] ___________ for messages. I [3] ___________ at 9.15, I have a shower and I [4] ___________ in my favourite clothes. Then I [5] ___________ (cereal). At ten o'clock, I brush my teeth, I [6] ___________ with my books, and I [7] ___________ on the bus. I have three classes and I go home to have lunch. I haven't got any homework! After dinner, I check my phone again and [8] ___________.

4 ☆☆☆ **Write about your ideal school day. Use Exercise 3 to help you.**

This is my ideal school day. I …

____

____

____

Explore it!

Guess the correct answer.

People in the UK *get dressed* / *have a shower* in eight minutes.

Find an interesting fact about daily routines in your country. Then send a question in an email to a classmate or ask them it in the next class.

READING

A profile

1 ★ **Read the profile. Is this sentence *T* (true) or *F* (false)?**

Dylan has got 25 hours of classes a week. ______

A day in the life of a

child actor

Dylan Roberts is 14, and he's a child actor. He makes films and doesn't go to school. He always has classes with special teachers called film tutors. Child actors usually have 15 hours of classes a week (schools have 25), but it isn't easy! Dylan often has lots of work to do.

Dylan talks about his typical day:

'I get up at six in the morning and get dressed. At 6.15, a car takes me to filming. I have breakfast at work and then I practise the day's filming for an hour. At 8.00, they do my hair and make-up and I get dressed in my film clothes. Filming starts at 9.00. Then, at 11.00, I have a break for half an hour. After that, I go to the tutor's room for classes. I don't have any homework. At 6.00 in the evening, I go home or to a hotel. I have a shower, have dinner, read my part of the film for tomorrow, and go to bed. It's a busy day!'

2 ★★ **Read the profile again and underline these words. Then check their meaning in a dictionary and complete the sentences.**

break busy filming ~~make-up~~ tutor

1. Here's the green _make-up_ for your eyes.
2. After three classes, we've got a ______ to have lunch.
3. All the actors are ready for ______ today.
4. I've got a ______ for extra English classes.
5. Our weekends are very ______ with lots of things to do!

3 ★★ **Read the profile again. Circle the correct answer.**

1. Dylan is a child actor. He *goes* / *(doesn't go)* to school.
2. Dylan's special teacher is a film *tutor* / *actor*.
3. A child actor *has* / *hasn't* got a lot of work to do.
4. Dylan has breakfast at *home* / *work*.
5. Dylan's first classes are *before* / *after* filming.
6. He hasn't got any *homework* / *breaks*.

4 ★★ **What's your opinion? Read the statements and write *Yes* or *No*.**

1. It's easy to be a child actor. ______
2. Fifteen hours of classes a week is a good idea. ______
3. Dylan's day is fun. ______
4. Not having homework is great. ______

LANGUAGE IN ACTION

Present simple: affirmative and negative

1 ☆ **Circle the correct options.**

1 Dylan is a child actor and he *make* / *makes* films.
2 Child actors *don't* / *doesn't* live at home when they are in a film.
3 They *eat* / *eats* dinner in a hotel.
4 We *study* / *studies* English.
5 Martha *have* / *has* breakfast at school.
6 Film tutors *teach* / *teaches* small classes.

2 ☆ **Write the third person singular of the present simple.**

have	watch	meet	go
1 has	2 ______	3 ______	4 ______

play	brush	do	hurry
5 ______	6 ______	7 ______	8 ______

3 ☆☆ **Complete the text with the present simple form of the verbs in brackets.**

Veera is 12. She [1] goes (go) to school in Finland, and her class [2] ______ (have got) 18 students. School [3] ______ (start) at 9.45 am and it [4] ______ (finish) at 2.45 pm. There are three or four classes a day. In Finland, students [5] ______ (not have got) homework or exams. Veera [6] ______ (have got) a lot of free time. After school, she [7] ______ (meet) her friends and they [8] ______ (go) to a sports club for lunch. Veera [9] ______ (love) sport and she [10] ______ (play) in the school football team. Her dream is to be a footballer!

Adverbs of frequency

4 ☆ **Match the adverbs of frequency with the ticks (✓) and cross (✗).**

1 always [c] a ✓✓
2 usually [ ] b ✗
3 often [ ] c ✓✓✓✓
4 sometimes [ ] d ✓
5 never [ ] e ✓✓✓

5 ☆ **Are these statements true for you? Write *T* (true) or *F* (false).**

1 I often do my homework with my friends. ______
2 I always check my phone when I wake up. ______
3 My best friend sometimes has lunch at my house. ______
4 I never go to bed late at the weekend. ______
5 I usually have lunch with my grandparents on Sundays. ______

6 ☆☆ **Write the words in the correct order to make sentences.**

1 makes / dad / often / dinner / My
My dad often makes dinner.
2 I / brush / after / teeth / always / my / breakfast
______
3 go / at / They / lunchtime / usually / home
______
4 sometimes / We / class / are / for / late
______
5 I / check / in / never / my / class / phone
______
6 does / in / the / Dan / park / homework / his / usually
______

VOCABULARY AND LISTENING

Leisure activities

1 ☆ Complete the leisure activity phrases.

1 play an instrument
2 go for a b_____e r_____e
3 read a book or a ma_____e
4 chat on_____e
5 play v_____o g_____s
6 make v_____s
7 take ph_____s
8 download s_____s
9 listen to m_____c
10 go sh_____g
11 hang out with fr_____s
12 watch _____V

2 ☆☆ Complete the sentences with the correct form of the phrases from Exercise 1.

1 Lucy often ___downloads songs___ from the internet – she doesn't buy CDs.
2 When I __________ with my friends, we talk for hours on our computers or phones.
3 I usually meet and __________ in the park after school.
4 Luke's sister plays the guitar, but he doesn't __________.
5 I use my phone to __________ – my friends are the actors. I sometimes put them on *YouTube*!
6 They never __________ now, they always find films and series online.

Street interviews

3 ☆ Listen to the interviews. Circle the correct answer. (2.01)

The interviews are about different …

a school activities.
b hobbies.
c instruments.

4 ☆☆ Listen again and number the activities in the photos in the order you hear them (1–3). (2.01)

a

b

c

5 ☆☆ Listen again and write *A* (Anja), *C* (Callum) or *D* (Debra). (2.01)

1 ___A___ does his/her hobby every day.
2 _____ and _____ do their hobbies at the weekend.
3 _____ does his/her hobby early in the morning.
4 _____ does his/her hobby with animals.
5 _____ uses the internet for his/her hobby.
6 _____ wants to do his/her hobby as a job.

6 ☆☆☆ Write about one of your hobbies. Use the questions below to help you.

Where? How often? When? Who with?

LANGUAGE IN ACTION

Present simple: questions

1 ☆ **Complete the questions with *Do* or *Does*. Then match them with answers a–f.**

1 ___Do___ you see your friends at the weekend? [b]
2 ______ your parents like the same music? [ ]
3 ______ your sister watch TV a lot? [ ]
4 ______ your cousin hang out with you? [ ]
5 ______ all your family play an instrument? [ ]
6 ______ this timetable have ten subjects? [ ]

a No, they don't.
b ~~Yes, I do~~.
c Yes, he does.
d Yes, we do.
e No, she doesn't.
f Yes, it does.

2 ☆☆ **Write the words in the correct order to make questions. Use the photos to help you.**

1 friends / you / online / Do / your / chat / with / ?
Do you chat online with your friends?
2 download / your / Does / best friend / songs / ?
______
3 go / for / Do / you / Sundays / a / bike / ride / on / ?
______
4 shopping / Do / you / go / a lot / ?
______
5 play / games / your / dad / video / Does / ?
______
6 your / books / Does / read / mum / ?
______

3 ☆☆ **Answer the questions in Exercise 2 for you. Use short answers.**

1 ______ 4 ______
2 ______ 5 ______
3 ______ 6 ______

Wh- questions

4 ☆ **(Circle) the correct question words.**

1 (*What*) / *When* do you do at the weekend?
2 *Where* / *Who* do you go after school?
3 *What* / *Who* does Emir have lunch with?
4 *Where* / *What* do you usually meet Ada?
5 *How often* / *Who* do they go shopping?
6 *Where* / *What time* do you wake up on Mondays?

5 ☆☆ **Complete the interview with a tennis player. Write questions using the words in brackets.**

JADE What time [1] *do you get up* (you / get up), Alina?
ALINA Very early! At seven o'clock.
JADE [2] ______ (you / get up) early at weekends, too?
ALINA No, not always.
JADE And how often [3] ______ (you / hang out) with friends?
ALINA I see my friends twice a week.
JADE [4] ______ (your friends / come) to your matches?
ALINA Yes, sometimes they do.
JADE Great! And [5] ______ (your parents / watch) you, too?
ALINA Yes. My dad comes to all my matches.
JADE Nice! And [6] ______ (other people / ask) you to do interviews?
ALINA No, they don't! I'm not famous!

WRITING

An article

1 ★ **Read the article. Circle the correct title.**

a What does Zev do at the weekend?

b What is Zev's daily routine?

Zev's from the USA. He's 12 years old. In his free time, he's a photographer. Zev's photos are of animals and objects. He often makes photo stories. He uses digital technology and his imagination.

1 This is a typical day in Zev's life. He always gets up at 7.00 and has a shower. At 7.30, he has breakfast. At 7.45, he brushes his teeth and packs his bag. He then goes to school at 8.00.

2 In the afternoon, Zev goes home. At 3.00, he usually has lunch and does his homework. He goes for a walk with his sister at 5.00 and looks for ideas for his photo stories.

3 From 6.30 to 8.00 in the evening, Zev makes his photo stories and puts them on his website. He sometimes chats online with his friends, but he never stays late. At 9.30, Zev goes to bed.

One day, I want to take photos like Zev!

2 Match topics a–c with paragraphs 1–3.

a description of Zev's evening routine ☐

b description of his morning routine ☐

c description of his afternoon routine ☐

3 ★ **Read the article again. What time does Zev do these things?**

1 gets up *7.00*

2 has breakfast ______

3 packs his bag ______

4 goes to school ______

5 has lunch ______

6 goes for a walk ______

7 makes his photo stories ______

8 goes to bed ______

4 ★ **Find and underline five adverbs of frequency in the article.**

5 ★★ **Rewrite the sentences with the correct punctuation.**

1 how does Zev make his photo stories

How does Zev make his photo stories?

2 zevs sister doesnt take photos

______

3 zevs friends look at his photo stories on his website

______

4 wow I think the photos are great

______

Write an article about someone's day.

PLAN

6 ★★ **Choose a person with a different daily routine from yours. It can be a friend or someone from your family. Decide what information to include in each paragraph. Use the information in Exercise 2 to help you.**

WRITE

7 ★★★ **Write your article. Remember to include the information in the correct order, the present simple, adverbs of frequency and correct punctuation from the *Useful language* box (see Student's Book, p29).**

CHECK

8 Do you ...

- include an interesting title with a question?
- introduce the person, their nationality and what they do?
- describe the person's morning, afternoon and evening routines?
- end the article with a sentence about you and your ambition?

2 REVIEW

VOCABULARY

1 Complete the text with the words in the box.

brush do dressed get go (x2) have pack shower up

I wake [1] ___________ at 6.30 and I [2] ___________ up at 7.00. Then I have a [3] ___________ and [4] ___________ my teeth. I get [5] ___________ in my school clothes and [6] ___________ my bag for school. At 7.30, I [7] ___________ breakfast with my mum and dad. I [8] ___________ to school at 8.30 and finish at 3.30. In the afternoon, I [9] ___________ my homework and then I've got some free time. In the evening, I have dinner with my parents and then I [10] ___________ to bed at about 10.00.

2 Match the verbs with the activities.

1 chat	☐	a	songs
2 download	☐	b	a bike ride
3 go for	☐	c	online
4 listen to	☐	d	a book or a magazine
5 hang out with	☐	e	music
6 read	☐	f	friends
7 go	☐	g	TV
8 watch	☐	h	shopping

LANGUAGE IN ACTION

3 Complete the sentences with the present simple form of the verbs in brackets.

1 I ___________ (not wake up) early at the weekend.
2 Martin ___________ (go) to school at 9.00 every day.
3 We ___________ (not do) our homework at school.
4 Tom's dad ___________ (make) videos of his birthday every year.
5 Isabela ___________ (not have) a big breakfast, only fruit.
6 Theo ___________ (not play) the guitar very often.

4 Circle the correct option.

1 Daniel ___________________ shopping with his mum.
   a sometimes goes   b goes sometimes
2 I ___________________ video games with my brother.
   a play often   b often play
3 My dad ___________________ to rock music!
   a listens never   b never listens
4 We ___________________ with friends at weekends.
   a always hang out   b hang out always
5 They finish their homework and they ___________________ TV.
   a watch often   b often watch

5 **Complete the questions and answers with the present simple form of the verbs in brackets. Add *Wh-* question words where necessary.**

1 A: ________ you ________ (brush) your teeth every day? B: Yes, I ________ .

2 A: ________ your mum ________ (pack) your bag for you? B: No, she ________ .

3 A: ________ your cousins ________ (play) an instrument? B: No, they ________ .

4 A: ________ time ________ Chris ________ (go) home? B: At 7.00.

5 A: ________ often ________ you ________ (read) a book? B: Every month.

6 A: ________ ________ you ________ (go) on Sundays? B: I often go to the park with my family.

CUMULATIVE LANGUAGE

6 **Complete the conversation with the missing words. Circle the correct options.**

ROSA [1] ________ do you do in your free time?

MIRA I [2] ________ my best friend or go with my brother for a bike ride.

ROSA [3] ________ you see your best friend every day?

MIRA Yes, most days. [4] ________ 's your best friend?

ROSA That's Susan, but I [5] ________ her all the time.

MIRA [6] ________ often do you see her?

ROSA It depends, but usually every weekend. We sometimes [7] ________ basketball on Saturdays.

MIRA Hey! I play, too. What [8] ________ do you meet on Saturdays?

ROSA Usually in the afternoon.

MIRA [9] ________ to hang out one Saturday?

ROSA Sure! [10] ________ your phone? Here's my number.

MIRA Yes, I [11] ________ . OK, great!

1 a What b Where
2 a meet usually b usually meet
3 a Does b Do
4 a Who b When
5 a don't see b doesn't see
6 a When b How
7 a play b plays
8 a often b time
9 a You want b Do you want
10 a Have got you b Have you got
11 a have b have got

3 SCHOOL DAYS

VOCABULARY

School subjects

1 ☆ Complete the subjects with the correct letters.

1 Eng l ish
2 Spani _ h
3 desig_ _nd techn_logy
4 m_ths
5 musi_
6 ar_
7 d_ama
8 geo_raphy
9 histor_
10 foo_ technology
11 P_
12 sci_nce
13 I_T

2 ☆ Write the correct school subjects from Exercise 1.

1 music

2 ______

3 ______

4 ______

5 ______

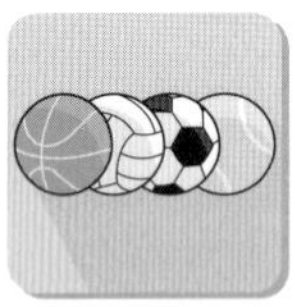

6 ______

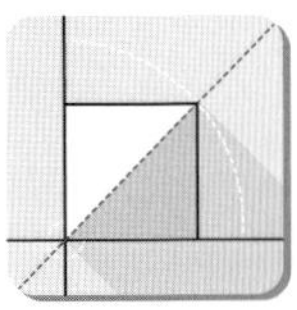

7 ______

8 ______

3 ☆☆ Write the subjects for the definitions.

1 You learn to play an instrument. music
2 You learn a language that people speak in lots of countries in South America. ______
3 You learn about people, countries and places. ______
4 You learn about things in the past. ______
5 You learn about numbers, shapes and space. ______
6 You learn a language that people speak in the UK and the USA. ______
7 You learn about food and what is good or bad to eat. ______
8 You do experiments. ______

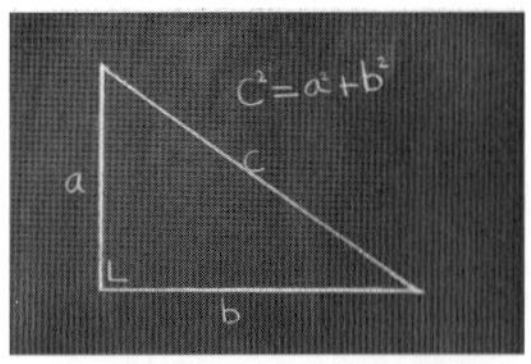

4 ☆☆ Write the names of these subjects in your language. Write *S* if they are similar to the words in English or *D* if they are different.

1 science ______ ______
2 geography ______ ______
3 drama ______ ______
4 art ______ ______

Explore it!

Guess the correct answer.

One school in Lucknow, India, has got a lot of students. How many students has it got?

a about 15,000 b about 27,000 c about 52,000

Find an interesting fact about school subjects in another country. Then send a question in an email to a classmate or ask them it in the next class.

READING

A webpage

1 ☆ **Read the webpage about schools in Singapore. Why don't teachers like posters in maths classrooms?**

____

HOME | STORIES | PHOTOS

SCHOOLS IN SINGAPORE

STUDENTS FROM SINGAPORE OFTEN GET VERY GOOD MARKS FOR MATHS AND SCIENCE IN INTERNATIONAL TESTS.

In maths lessons, students can use technology to answer the different maths problems. Their answers go on the whiteboard at the front of the class. All students can see and talk about their classmates' answers.

A lot of maths classrooms don't have posters on the walls. Teachers don't think posters help students learn.

Students can't talk to each other a lot. They work alone, but they can ask the teacher questions when they don't understand something.

In science classes, students can work on their projects once a week. In one class, they can build a robotic arm and in another class students can make a small radio.

In many secondary schools in Singapore, students don't do a lot of drama, language, music or art. Some teachers say, 'Art subjects aren't very important. Students need to be good at science and maths. They need these subjects for their adult life'. Is this a good or a bad idea? What do you think?

2 ☆☆ **Read the webpage again and underline these words. Then check their meaning in a dictionary and complete the sentences.**

~~adult~~ alone build marks whiteboard

1 In many countries, you're an _adult_ when you're 18.

2 My teacher always writes the answers on the ______.

3 I never get good ______ in geography. Maps are difficult!

4 We want to ______ a robot for our project.

5 **A:** Do you need help?
B: No, thanks. I always do my homework ______.

3 ☆☆ **Answer the questions.**

1 What subjects are students from Singapore often good at?
maths and science

2 What do teachers show on the whiteboard?
______

3 How do students work in maths classes?
______

4 How often do students work on science projects?
______

5 Which subjects are not very important in many schools?
______

4 ☆☆☆ **Answer the questions with your own ideas.**

1 'Art subjects aren't very important.' What do you think?
______

2 Which subjects do you think are important? Why?
______

LANGUAGE IN ACTION

can for ability and permission

1 ☆ **Circle the options that are true for you.**

1 In our classes, we *can* / *can't* put posters on the walls.

2 At break time, we *can* / *can't* play and talk to friends.

3 We *can* / *can't* talk in science classes.

4 We *can* / *can't* build interesting things for our projects.

5 Sometimes we *can* / *can't* work in groups in our English classes.

2 ☆☆ **Complete the sentences. Use *can/can't* and the verbs in brackets.**

1 My dad ___can't sing___ because he hasn't got a good voice, but he ______________ amazing pictures. (sing / draw)

2 My cousin ______________ good photos but she ______________ videos. She's really bad at it! (take / make)

3 My mum ______________ salsa quite well and she ______________ the guitar, too. She's really good at it! (dance / play)

4 My little brother's four. He ______________ English very well but he ______________ it. (speak / read)

3 ☆☆ **Complete the texts with *can/can't* and the verbs in brackets.**

RAJ

My favourite subject is history. I like it because we [1] ___can work___ (work) in groups – it's great when we [2] ______________ (do) projects together. But we work alone when we have an exam – we [3] ______________ (talk). After the exam we usually have a break and we [4] ______________ (hang out) with friends.

PAULA

My favourite teacher is Mark, our geography teacher. I like his classes because we [5] ______________ (ask) questions when we need to. We have options, too: sometimes we [6] ______________ (choose) our homework and we [7] ______________ (bring) interesting things to class. But we [8] ______________ (be) late – Mark doesn't like that!

4 ☆☆ **Write questions and short answers with *can*.**

1 students / check their phone / in class? (✗)
Can students check their phone in class?
No, they can't.

2 students / ask questions / in class? (✓)
____
____

3 Kate / play the piano? (✓)
____
____

4 María / speak two languages? (✗)
____
____

5 students / work in groups / in maths classes? (✓)
____
____

6 you / do ballet? (✗)
____
____

5 ☆☆ **Are these statements true for you? Write *T* (true) or *F* (false).**

1 I can speak two languages. ________

2 I can dance salsa. ________

3 I can ride a bike. ________

4 I can play the guitar. ________

5 I can sing. ________

VOCABULARY AND LISTENING

Places in a school

1 ★ **Read the definitions. Then circle the correct places in the spidergram.**

1 You can do outdoor sports here.
2 You can buy and eat food here.
3 You can do PE here.
4 Teachers can plan their lessons here.
5 You can leave your bag here.
6 You can read books and study here.
7 You can wash your hands here.

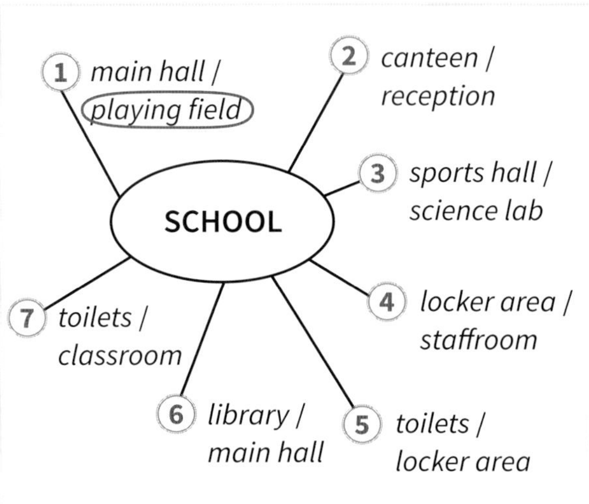

2 ★★ **Complete the text with places from Exercise 1.**

Mondays!

I don't like my timetable on Mondays! At 8.45 I go to [1] *reception* and say hello to my aunt – she works at the school. Then I go to the [2] __________ and put my sports shoes in my locker. After that, my class goes to the [3] __________ and we do experiments. I don't like science! At break time, I usually go to the [4] __________ for some food. Then we have PE in the [5] __________ and then lunch. In the afternoon, it's music and drama. At 4.15, we go to the [6] __________ and get a book to read – that's OK because I like books, but I'm always happy on Mondays at 4.30 because I can go home!

A radio programme

3 3.01 ★★ **Listen and number the places in the order you hear them (1–6).**

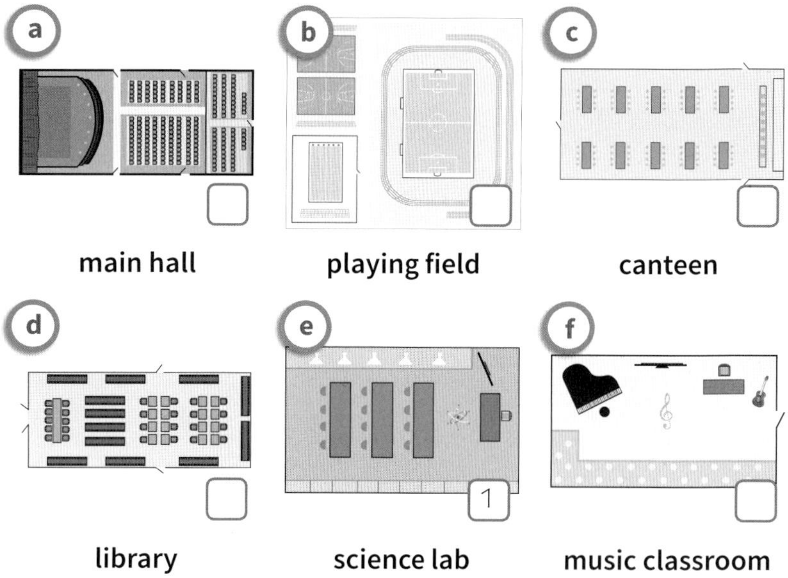

4 3.01 ★★ **Listen again. Are the sentences *T* (true) or *F* (false)?**

1 Alex likes the science lab. T
2 He likes the magazines from the library. ____
3 Alex's favourite subject is PE. ____
4 The music classroom is Alex's favourite place. ____
5 Marina has lunch in the canteen. ____
6 She likes all the places in the school. ____

LANGUAGE IN ACTION

Verb forms: (*don't*) *like, don't mind, love, hate* + *-ing*

1 ★ **Match the verbs with the symbols.**

1 love [b] 2 like [ ] 3 don't mind [ ]
4 don't like [ ] 5 hate [ ]

a  b  c  d  e 

2 ★★ **Write sentences with the correct form of the verbs.**

1 I / like / go / to the music club
I like going to the music club.

2 We / hate / have / lots of homework
____

3 Tariq / not mind / do / sport in the sports hall
____

4 Gina / love / play / football / on the playing field
____

5 They / not like / learn / history
____

3 ★★ **Complete the text with the correct form of the verbs in brackets.**

I've got a twin brother but we're very different! He [1] *hates getting up* (hate / get up) early but I [2] ________ (not mind / do) it for school. He [3] ________ (love / do) sport and I [4] ________ (like / play) video games. I [5] ________ (not like / go) to parties. I [6] ________ (like / stay) at home. My brother [7] ________ (love / hang out) with his friends and [8] ________ (have) a good time. He [9] ________ (not mind / study) sometimes, but he doesn't love it. I [10] ________ (love / learn) new things, especially about science.

Object pronouns

4 ★ **Complete the table with the object pronouns.**

Subject	I	you	he	she	it	we	they
Object	1 *me*	2 ____	3 ____	4 ____	5 ____	6 ____	7 ____

5 ★ **Circle the correct option.**

1 **A:** Do you like drama? **B:** Yes, I like (*it*) / *them*.
2 Mr Patel isn't at reception. Can you phone *her* / *him*?
3 I've got a problem. Can you help *me* / *it*, please?
4 Is Amaya here? I can't see *you* / *her*.
5 **A:** Do you like video games? **B:** I hate *it* / *them*.
6 What classes have we got today? Can you give *us* / *you* the timetable, please?

6 ★★ **Look at the pictures and then complete the text with the correct subject or object pronouns.**

Me (Josh)

Lucas

Lucas' mum

Spanish

I'm Josh, and Lucas is my best friend. [1] *We* (+) 're in the same class and [2] ______ ( ) lives near [3] ______ ( ). Lucas' mum is Spanish. [4] ______ ( ) speaks Spanish with [5] ______ ( ) at home, but [6] ______ ( ) speak English with [7] ______ (+). We learn Spanish at school and Lucas helps [8] ______ ( ) with my homework. Spanish is difficult, but I like [9] ______ ( ).

WRITING

A description

1 ☆ **Read Sanjiv's description. Does he like his school?**

____

My school

1 *Courses and subjects*

I study at a very big school. Students can do different courses <u>such as</u> science or arts. I'm on the science course. I study English, maths and science and technology subjects, <u>like</u> computer science. That's my favourite subject.

2 ______________________

I really like the teachers. They teach regular classes, but they also teach some after-school clubs, <u>like</u> astronomy and dance. I like being with my teachers after class.

3 ______________________

We have six lessons a day and homework. I don't mind doing some homework, but I don't like a lot of it! I really like working with my classmates on group projects. I don't like working alone!

4 ______________________

Our school has got great places for lessons and activities. <u>For example</u>, we've got a big sports building, a canteen, an ICT room and three science labs. I love studying here.

2 ☆ **Write the correct heading for each paragraph in the description.**

Great teachers ~~Courses and subjects~~
School places School routine

3 ☆ **Read the description again. Then complete the text below with the phrases in the box.**

computer science doing a lot of homework ~~the teachers at his school~~ working alone

Sanjiv likes [1] *the teachers at his school* and [2] ______________________. He doesn't like [3] ______________________ or [4] ______________________.

4 ☆ **Look at the <u>underlined</u> words and phrases in Sanjiv's description. What does he use them for? Circle the correct answer.**

a to join ideas
b to show different times
c to give examples

Write a description of your school.

PLAN

5 ☆☆ **Make a spidergram of your school in your notebook and use the plan below.**

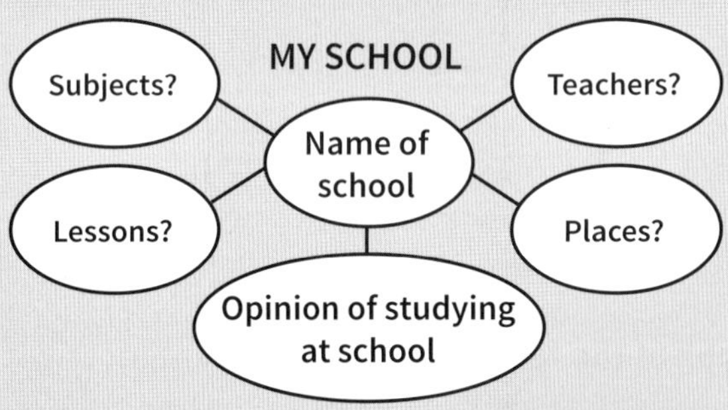

6 **Decide what information to include in each paragraph. Use your spidergram and the information in Exercise 2 to help you.**

WRITE

7 ☆☆☆ **Write your description. Remember to include four paragraphs, *can/can't* and expressions from the *Useful language* box (see Student's Book, p41).**

CHECK

8 **Do you …**

- give the name of the school in the opening sentence?
- include all of the information from your spidergram?
- give your opinion about studying at the school in your closing sentence?

3 REVIEW

VOCABULARY

1 Complete the school subjects.

1 Languages: E_ _ _ _ _ _ _, S_ _ _ _ _ _
2 Numbers: m_ _ _ _
3 The past: h_ _ _ _ _ _
4 Countries: g_ _ _ _ _ _ _ _
5 In a lab: s_ _ _ _ _ _ _, f_ _ _ t_ _ _ _ _ _ _ _ _
6 Art subjects: d_ _ _ _ _ and t_ _ _ _ _ _ _ _ _ _,
d_ _ _ _, m_ _ _ _, a_ _
7 Sport: p_ _ _ _ _ _ _ e_ _ _ _ _ _ _ _
8 ICT: i_ _ _ _ _ _ _ _ _ _ and
c_ _ _ _ _ _ _ _ _ _ _ _ _ t_ _ _ _ _ _ _ _

2 Find 12 places in a school in the word search.

R	O	L	O	C	K	E	R	A	R	E	A	N
E	P	I	C	O	M	E	C	H	I	B	J	S
C	A	B	S	T	A	F	F	R	O	O	M	P
E	N	R	E	R	I	H	A	L	F	K	J	O
P	L	A	Y	I	N	G	F	I	E	L	D	R
T	H	R	T	E	H	I	T	P	V	A	I	T
I	B	Y	O	C	A	N	T	E	E	N	C	S
O	C	E	I	H	L	A	C	T	E	R	T	H
N	O	S	L	E	L	O	R	R	N	E	R	A
S	C	I	E	N	C	E	L	A	B	Y	O	L
S	U	Y	T	T	H	I	P	R	M	E	O	L
C	L	A	S	S	R	O	O	M	O	P	M	S

LANGUAGE

3 Look at the table. Complete the sentences with *can/can't* and the correct verbs.

 **Jon**	✓	✗	✓
 **Lisa**	✗	✓	✓

1 Jon ______________ the guitar.
2 Lisa ______________ the guitar.
3 ______________ Jon ______________ songs in English? ______________, he ______________.
4 ______________ Lisa ______________ songs in English? ______________, she ______________.
5 Jon and Lisa ______________ Spanish.

4 Look at the symbols. Write sentences using (*don't*) *like*, *don't mind*, *love*, *hate* + *-ing*.

1 We /  / talk to / our teachers ______________________

2 I /  / do / homework ______________________

3 She /  / listen / to music ______________________

4 They /  / have / lunch at school ______________________

5 He /  / be / late for class ______________________

5 Match questions 1–6 with answers a–f.

1 Does Tom like football? ☐

2 Does Berta play video games? ☐

3 Can you help Suzi? ☐

4 Is Harry in your class? ☐

5 Is this party for you and your friends? ☐

6 Do you like reading? ☐

a No, it isn't for us!

b No, he hates it!

c I don't mind it.

d Yes, she loves them.

e Yes, I can help her.

f Yes, he's with me.

CUMULATIVE LANGUAGE

6 Complete the conversation with the missing words. Circle the correct options.

DENIZ Hi, Kate! [1] ________ football today?

KATE No, I [2] ________ . It's Wednesday today.

DENIZ When [3] ________ practice?

KATE On Tuesdays and Thursdays, and at the weekend [4] ________ have matches.

DENIZ Oh! And [5] ________ your parents watch your matches?

KATE It depends. [6] ________ come and see me.

DENIZ Hey, [7] ________ do we finish class today?

KATE At three o'clock! It's Wednesday, remember?

DENIZ Oh, great! Harry and I [8] ________ for a bike ride after school on Wednesdays.

KATE [9] ________ Harry now?

DENIZ He's in the library. He [10] ________ a maths project to finish.

KATE Well, I love [11] ________ . [12] ________ I go with you?

DENIZ Sure!

	a	b	c
1	Have you got	You has got	You have
2	hasn't	haven't got	haven't
3	do you have	have you	you have
4	always we	we always	it always
5	does	do	are
6	They sometimes	Them sometimes	Sometimes them
7	when	who	what
8	go usually	usually goes	usually go
9	What's	Where's	Who's
10	's got	've got	haven't
11	cycling	cycle	cycles
12	Do	Can	Have

4 YOU ARE WHAT YOU EAT

VOCABULARY

Food and drink

1 ☆ Complete the table with the words in the box.

~~apples~~ bananas beans cheese chicken eggs fish fizzy drink water

Food from plants	Food from animals	Drinks
apples	______	______
______	______	______
______	______	
	______	

2 ☆☆ Circle the correct answers in the quiz.

ALL ABOUT FOOD AND DRINK

1 Which food is NOT usually a cake?
   a chicken **b** chocolate
2 Which of these is NOT protein?
   a meat **b** carrots
3 Which of these is NOT from fruit?
   a juice **b** chocolate
4 Which of these is NOT from a plant?
   a meat **b** rice

3 ☆☆ Complete the food words in the text.

I'm Zara from Malaysia. I usually have kaya toast with [1]e g g s for breakfast. I have lunch at school. Lunch is usually rice and [2]me_ _ or [3]ch_ _ _ _ _ curry with vegetables. I drink [4]ju_ _ _ made from orange and purple [5]ca_ _ _ _ _ and red [6]ap_ _ _ _. It's yummy! My mum cooks dinner. I love her [7]fi_ _ curry with [8]be_ _ _. We always drink [9]w_ _ _ _.

4 ☆☆☆ What is your favourite food for breakfast, lunch and dinner? Write about what you eat. Use Exercise 3 to help you.

I usually have ...
______
______
______

Explore it!

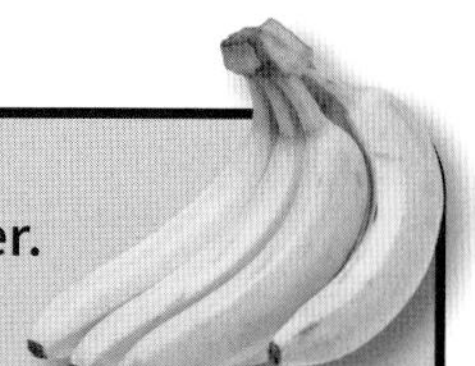

Guess the correct answer.

Which country grows millions of bananas?

a the UK b Ecuador c China

Find an interesting fact about food in your country. Then send a question in an email to a classmate or ask them it in the next class.

READING

An article

1 ☆ Read the article and match the foods in the box with the photos (1–3).

blinis	herring with potatoes	mooncakes

Welcome to my festival!

1 ____________

2 ____________

3 ____________

Hugo: Midsummer Eve, Sweden

I love this festival in June. It's at the start of the school holidays. We go to the countryside and in the morning we get some flowers for our hair. Then we dance to traditional music. Lunch is outside, and it's big! We always eat herring (a type of fish) with potatoes. Later, people play instruments and dance all night!

Mei Lin: Moon Festival, China

My favourite festival is in September, when we can see the first full moon of the month. We make paper lights and go to the park. And of course, we eat a mooncake or two! These are small round cakes (like the moon!) that have different fillings. I like the chocolate one. We give them to our friends and eat them together.

Daria: Maslenitsa Pancake Festival, Russia

This great festival is in February. We have fun activities for seven days! We do some sports, play music, dance and eat lots of food. I love having blinis. They are Russian pancakes made with butter, eggs and milk. We eat them with different toppings. My favourite topping is salmon and cream cheese. Yummy!

2 ☆☆ Read the article again and <u>underline</u> these words. Then check their meaning in a dictionary and complete the sentences.

countryside	fillings	full moon	pancakes	~~toppings~~

1 What are your favourite *toppings* on a pizza? I love extra cheese!
2 Once a month, we can see the ________ in the sky. It's completely round.
3 *Empanadas* are popular in South America. They have different ________ inside, such as meat or vegetables.
4 I love going to the ________ and looking at the trees and flowers.
5 We need milk and butter to make ________ .

3 ☆☆ Read the article again and complete the table.

Festival	Country	Month	Special food
Midsummer Eve	Sweden	1 *June*	2 ________
Moon	3 ________	4 ________	mooncakes
Maslenitsa	5 ________	February	6 ________

4 ☆☆☆ Answer the questions with your own ideas.

1 Which of the festivals is your favourite? Why?

____

2 Think of a festival in your country. When is it? What food do you have?

____

LANGUAGE IN ACTION

Countable and uncountable nouns

1 ☆ Write the correct headings in the table: *Countable* or *Uncountable*.

1 ______	2 ______
cheese water bread	apple egg tomato
rice	______
______	______
______	______

2 ☆ Complete the table in Exercise 1 with the words in the box.

bean carrot chocolate fish ~~rice~~ taco

A/An, some/any

3 ☆ Circle the correct options.

1 We use *a* or *an* with *countable* / *uncountable* nouns.
2 We use *some* and *any* with *singular* / *plural* countable nouns and uncountable nouns.
3 We use *some* in *affirmative* / *negative* sentences.
4 We use *any* in *affirmative* / *negative* sentences and questions.

4 ☆☆ Complete the sentences with the words in the box.

~~apple~~ chocolate eggs juice sandwich

1 Have you got an *apple* for your snack?
2 We haven't got any ______ for an omelette.
3 I'm hungry. Have you got a ______ for me?
4 Drink some ______ with your breakfast.
5 Can we have some ______ after dinner?

5 ☆☆ Complete the conversation with *a*, *an*, *some*, or *any*.

KIM What can we have for dinner? Have we got [1] *any* rice?
DAN No, we haven't got [2] ______ rice, but we've got [3] ______ pasta.
KIM Pasta with cheese! Have we got [4] ______ cheese?
DAN No. I can see [5] ______ tomato and [6] ______ egg, but that's all! Let's go to the shop.
KIM OK. Can you write a list? We need [7] ______ cheese, [8] ______ milk and [9] ______ tomatoes. Is that all?
DAN No. We haven't got [10] ______ drinks. We need [11] ______ juice.
KIM Right! And [12] ______ chocolate!

6 ☆☆☆ What is your favourite dinner? What have you got at home to make it and what do you need? Write sentences with *a / an*, *some* and *any*.

I want ______ for dinner.
I've got ______
I haven't got ______
I need ______

VOCABULARY AND LISTENING

Adjectives

1 ☆ Complete the adjectives with the missing vowels. Then match adjectives 1, 5, 7 and 10 with the photos (a–d).

1 h*o*t [d]	6 n_c_
2 d_l_c___s	7 c_ld [ ]
3 _nh__lthy	8 h__lthy
4 d_sg_st_ng	9 fr_sh
5 sw__t [ ]	10 s_lty [ ]

a

b

c

d

2 ☆☆ Circle the correct options.

1 Careful! The milk is *cold* / (*hot*)!
2 I don't like beans. They're *nice* / *disgusting*!
3 Ice cream is perfect for a hot day. It's *hot* / *cold* and *sweet* / *salty*.
4 Water is a *healthy* / *unhealthy* drink, but fizzy drinks are *healthy* / *unhealthy*.
5 I like having *disgusting* / *fresh* fruit for breakfast.

A quiz

4.01 **3 ☆ Listen to the family. Do they answer all the questions in the quiz?**

____

4.01 **4 ☆ Listen again. Match the foods (1–3) with the restaurants (a–c) .**

1

kebab

2

tacos

3
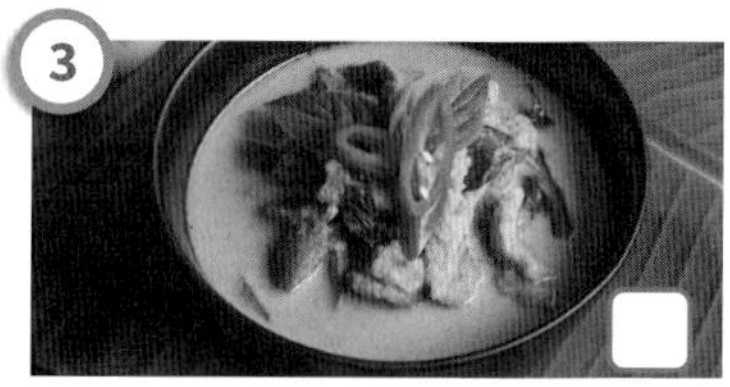
curry

a La Cantina   b Kumkapi   c Bangkok Garden

5 ☆☆ Listen again. Are the sentences *T* (true) or *F* (false)?

1 The restaurants in the quiz are new. ___T___
2 The names of the restaurants are in the first question. ______
3 The girl thinks Turkish food is sweet. ______
4 'Fresh' and 'healthy' describe two of the three types of food. ______
5 The boy thinks kebabs are delicious. ______
6 The children both want to go to the Mexican restaurant. ______

6 ☆☆☆ Do you prefer Mexican, Turkish or Thai food? Look on the internet for more information about these types of food. Write your ideas.

I prefer ________ *because it's* ________

LANGUAGE IN ACTION

there is/isn't, there are/aren't

1 ★ Look at the picture of the restaurant. Circle the correct options.

1 There is / *isn't* a picture on the wall.
2 There *is some* / *isn't any* water in the glasses.
3 There *is some* / *isn't any* food on the tables.
4 There *are some* / *aren't any* children.
5 There *are* / *aren't* eight people.
6 There *is* / *isn't* a window in the picture.

2 ★★ Look at the picture and complete the questions and answers with the correct form of *there is* / *there are*.

1 Is there any juice?
Yes, there is.
2 ________ any bananas?
________, there ________.
3 ________ any tomatoes?
________, there ________.
4 ________ any cheese?
________, there ________.
5 ________ any milk?
________, there ________.

much/many, a lot of

3 ★★ Circle the correct options.

My sister loves cooking and she's got [1]*a lot of* / *much* ideas for delicious meals. I like cooking, too, but I haven't got [2]*many* / *much* time to help her. She often uses [3]*a lot of* / *much* fruit and vegetables. She loves healthy food. Tonight, she wants to make pasta for dinner, but there isn't [4]*many* / *much* pasta and there aren't [5]*many* / *much* tomatoes in the fridge. The good thing is that there are [6]*a lot of* / *much* restaurants near home!

4 ★★ Complete the questions in the quiz with *much* or *many*. Then circle the correct answers.

HOW MUCH DO YOU KNOW?

1 How ________ milk is there in 1kg of cheese?
a two litres b five litres

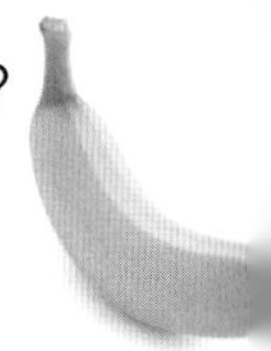

2 How ________ water is there in a banana?
a 74% b 90%

3 How ________ sugar is there in an average glass of orange juice?
a about 21 g b about 50 g

4 How ________ coffee beans are there in a 1kg bag of coffee?
a about 1,500 b about 8,800

5 ★★★ Look in your fridge and answer the questions.

1 How much fruit is there?
____
2 How many vegetables are there?
____

WRITING

A description

1 ★ **Look at the menus and read the description. Which menu is from Eva's favourite place, a or b?**

My favourite place to eat

by Eva García

1 My name's Eva [1](and) / *but* I'm from Chile. My favourite place to eat is a small café called Buenas Migas. I go there every Friday with my best friend and our parents.

2 Buenas Migas is near my house. There isn't a lot of space inside the café [2]*and / or* it hasn't got many tables, [3]*or / but* there are some more tables outside. We sit outside when the weather's nice.

3 You can eat different sandwiches, and they're all delicious! They've got egg, cheese, chicken [4]*but / or* meat sandwiches and they're all healthy. My favourite is the egg sandwich.

4 To drink, you can have water, fizzy drinks [5]*but / or* juice. Their orange and carrot juice is always fresh. It's definitely my favourite drink!

a

b

2 ★★ **(Circle) the correct options in the description.**

3 ★★ **(Circle) the correct options.**

We use [1]*but / or* when there is a choice (usually between two things).

We use [2]*but / and* to contrast different information.

We use [3]*or / and* to add similar information.

4 ★★ **Read the description again. Match topics a–d with paragraphs 1–4.**

a food (including your favourite) [3]

b introduction: who you are, what the description is about [ ]

c drinks (including your favourite) [ ]

d the place: where it is and what it is like [ ]

Write a description of your favourite place to eat.

PLAN

5 ★★ **Make notes about your favourite place to eat. Say where it is, when you go there and what it is like. Decide what information to include in each paragraph. Use the information in Exercise 4 to help you.**

WRITE

6 ★★★ **Write your description. Remember to include four paragraphs, *there is/are*, countable and uncountable nouns and expressions from the *Useful language* box (see Student's Book, p53).**

CHECK

7 **Do you …**

- introduce yourself and say where you are from and the name of your favourite place?
- say what is your favourite type of food and drink?
- use adjectives to describe food?

4 REVIEW

VOCABULARY

1 Write the food or drink words. Use the picture to help you.

1 They are a vegetable. They are long and orange. _ _ _ _ _ _ _

2 You can make cheese from this drink. _ _ _ _

3 It's usually brown and it's sweet. It's made from cacao. _ _ _ _ _ _ _ _ _

4 It's usually on top of pizzas. _ _ _ _ _ _

5 They come from chickens. _ _ _ _

6 It's a yellow fruit. There are lots in Ecuador. _ _ _ _ _ _

7 You make this drink with fruit or vegetables. _ _ _ _ _

8 It's a drink, but we also use it to have a shower. _ _ _ _ _

2 Match the opposites.

1 healthy ☐ a disgusting
2 delicious ☐ b sweet
3 cold ☐ c unhealthy
4 salty ☐ d hot

LANGUAGE IN ACTION

3 (Circle) the correct option: *C* (countable) or *U* (uncountable).

1 apple *C / U*
2 cheese *C / U*
3 water *C / U*
4 sandwich *C / U*
5 bread *C / U*
6 milk *C / U*
7 potato *C / U*
8 chocolate *C / U*
9 banana *C / U*
10 bean *C / U*

4 Complete the text with *a*, *some* or *any*.

It's my mum's birthday today and my dad and I want to make her a nice meal. We haven't got [1] __________ chicken, but we've got [2] __________ meat to cook with [3] __________ rice. There's [4] __________ bottle of water in the fridge and we've got [5] __________ fruit juice, too. There are [6] __________ carrots and [7] __________ tomatoes as well. We've got [8] __________ book for my mum. She loves reading.

5 Complete the dialogue with the words and phrases in the box.

Are there any	How many	Is there	
much	some	there are	There aren't

LUIS Let's make dinner.

ANDREA OK. We can cook some chicken with vegetables. [1] __________ vegetables?

LUIS Yes, [2] __________. We've got three carrots and some tomatoes.

ANDREA [3] __________ tomatoes are there? I need three.

LUIS [4] __________ three – only two.

ANDREA OK. [5] __________ any cheese? We can have the tomatoes with some cheese.

LUIS Yes, there's [6] __________ cheese!

ANDREA Great. And how [7] __________ chicken is there?

LUIS A lot! We can eat chicken for dinner, breakfast and lunch!

CUMULATIVE LANGUAGE

6 Complete the conversation with the missing words. (Circle) the correct options.

VICTOR Mum, what [1] __________ for dinner?

MUM There's [2] __________ soup and fish. Do you want that?

VICTOR Yes, I'm hungry! And [3] __________ can I have to drink?

MUM [4] __________ some fizzy water.

VICTOR Have we got any juice? I don't like [5] __________ fizzy water.

MUM Have a look in the fridge. I think there [6] __________ two bottles of juice there.

VICTOR Yes! And it's orange juice – delicious! Do you want some juice, too?

MUM No, thanks. I [7] __________ like it much. I prefer water. [8] __________ any apples for after your dinner?

VICTOR No, there [9] __________ any, but there are some bananas. I [10] __________ eat those.

MUM You're hungry! There's [11] __________ food, and you can eat all of it!

VICTOR OK, Mum. Yes, I'm really hungry!

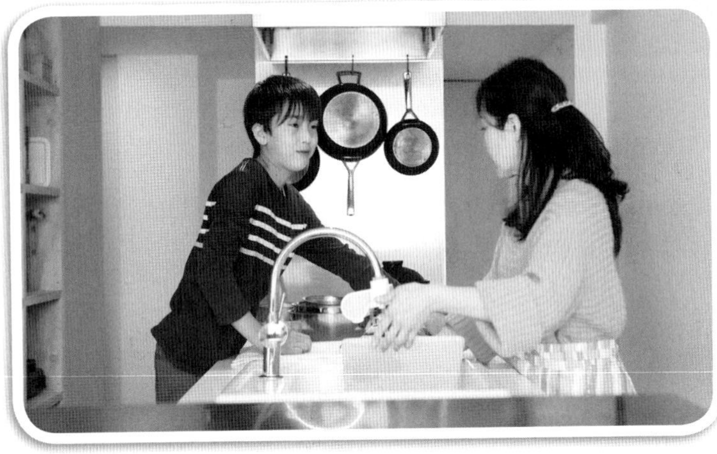

	a	b	c
1	there is	is there	are there
2	some	a	an
3	where	what	when
4	There are	There is	There has
5	drink	drinking	drinks
6	are	have	is
7	do	don't	'm not
8	Are there	Is there	Are they
9	aren't	isn't	haven't
10	am	do	can
11	much	a lot of	many

EXAM TIPS: Reading skills

Reading Part 2: Multiple matching

In this part of the test you have to read three short texts about three different people. They are all about the same topic. The title tells you what the topic is. There are seven questions. They all start with: ***Which person …?*** **The answer to each question is the name of one of the three people. To answer the question you need to circle the correct answer, A, B or C.**

Example:

	Tim	*Tom*	*Ted*
Which person did a lot of sport at school?	*A*	*B*	*C*

Exam guide: Multiple matching

- Start by reading the title of the text so you know what the topic is.
- Read all the questions carefully and underline the important words. This helps when you look for the same information in the texts.

  Example:

  Which person did a lot of sport at school?
- Now read the three texts for the first time without stopping. Maybe you see information similar to the questions, but read to the end.
- Now read the first question again. Then look at the texts to find which person says this. Maybe you remember something from one of the texts, so go to that text first to check. If not, just read from the beginning until you find what you need.
- When you find the correct answer, underline the words in the text with the same meaning as the question. Write the number of the question next to the part you underlined. Then circle your answer, A, B or C.

  Example:

  When I was a teenager I was in the school hockey, athletics and swimming teams.
- Then read the next question and do the same until you finish.
- You don't lose points for a wrong answer, so always circle a letter, even if you're not sure.

REMEMBER!

When you look for the answer, remember that the words in the question are probably different from the words in the text, but the meaning is the same. So if you see a word in the text that is the same as a word in the question, it is not automatically the correct answer.

Example:

I did a lot of sport after school when I was younger.

This is **NOT** the correct answer to the example question, because the meaning is different from the question.

Reading Part 2 practice: Multiple matching

1 **Underline the most important words in these questions.**

0 Which person does a lot of sport at the weekend?

Which person

1 loves trying new activities after school?

2 has got a lot of online friends?

3 reads science and nature magazines on the internet?

4 wants to study art or drama at school next year?

5 hasn't got any aunts, uncles or cousins?

6 doesn't like living in a big city?

> **Tip!** Underlining the most important words in the questions helps you to remember the information you need to find in the text.

2 **Match words 1–9 with their opposites in the box.**

after	boring	difficult	evening	finish	good	hate	late	short	~~small~~

0 big ___small___

1 easy ______ 4 long ______ 7 morning ______

2 early ______ 5 start ______ 8 fun ______

3 love ______ 6 before ______ 9 bad ______

> **Tip!** When reading the text, look for words or phrases which are opposites (often with a negative verb) or synonyms of the words in the question.

3 **Read the text and match the words in bold with the synonyms 1–9.**

One place in my **road** that's very popular with **young people** is the skate park. Some of my friends spend all their **leisure time** there. There is also a **big** sports centre near me, with some good **courses**, like swimming and dancing. **Many** of my friends **tell me** they would like to go there too, but the **price** is too high. I **travel** to a cheaper gym but it's not very near my house and so it's **difficult** to get to.

0 street ___road___ 2 large ______ 4 free time ______ 6 hard ______ 8 cost ______

1 a lot ______ 3 say ______ 5 teenagers ______ 7 go ______ 9 classes ______

4 **Choose the option, A or B, which has the same meaning as the question.**

0 Which person has a lot of homework to do?

(A) I spend about two hours every night on school work.

B In my school the teachers don't usually give us much homework.

1 Which person isn't happy about their hair colour?

A I've got red hair but I don't mind. It's the same as Ed Sheeran's!

B Everyone in my family has got blonde hair. It's boring. I want to be different.

2 Which person reads information about science on the internet?

A There is so much interesting stuff to read online these days, especially science articles.

B I love reading my dad's science magazines. He buys them every month.

3 Which person doesn't mind getting up early in the morning?

A I have to get up at seven so I'm not late for school, but that isn't a problem.

B I'm glad when it's Saturday and I can get up late.

4 Which person thinks living in the country is boring?

A People say that the country is boring but I think there's lots to do.

B I'm happy I live in the city. I'm sure it's more exciting than being in a village.

EXAM TIPS: Writing skills

Writing Part 6: Writing a short email or note

In this part of the test, you have to write a short email or note of 25 words or more. Under the instructions there is a space to write the text.

The instructions in the test tell you exactly what you need to do.

Example:

You want to ***go to the cinema*** *with* ***your friend*** *Jan on* ***Saturday****. Write an email to Jan.*

The instructions also explain three things you need to include in the text. For example:

In the email:

- **ask** Jan to **go to the cinema** with you
- say **what film** you want to see
- say **where** you can **meet**.

Exam guide: Writing a short email or note

- It is important to include all the points from the instructions in the text. It is also better to keep them in the same order as in the instructions.
- The text needs
  - an opening sentence
  - three sentences, one for each point
  - a sentence to close (for example a question asking your friend's opinion)
  - (in an email) your name at the end.
- When you finish, read the text again and count the number of words. If you have included all the information from the plan above, the text should be at least 25 words. If it's more, that's OK. If you haven't written 25 words, go back and check that you have included all the points and the opening and the closing sentences.

Writing Part 7: Writing a short story

In this part of the test, you have to write a short story of 35 words or more. To help you there are three pictures. You write the story they show. Under the pictures there is a space to write your story.

Exam guide: Writing a short story

- Don't start writing immediately. Look at the pictures for a minute and decide what the story is about. A good way to plan a story is to think about *Who? Where? When?* and *What?*
- Give any people in the picture a name. Then write any useful vocabulary you want to use (nouns, verbs, adjectives, etc.) next to each picture.
- Decide how to start (e.g. *One day/Yesterday*). Use the past tense when you write your story.
- When you finish writing, count the words. You need to write at least 35 words.

REMEMBER!

You will be given a piece of paper to make notes. Use it to plan your writing.

Writing Parts 6 & 7 practice: An email or note; a short story

1 Match the phrases from a text message with the right category A–C.

> **Tip!** For this part of the test, try to use different phrases for inviting and suggesting ideas.

A opening   B inviting or suggesting   C closing phrase

0 *I'd like to see the new X-men film.* B
1 What do you think? ______
2 Do you want to go swimming this afternoon? ______
3 Let me know soon. ______
4 Hey ______
5 Shall we meet at the bus stop at seven? ______
6 Hi Jan ______
7 We can try the new pool. ______
8 How about going to the cinema on Saturday? ______

2 Order the words to make sentences from an email.

0 *cheap / to / a / go / restaurant / Let's / .* Let's go to a cheap restaurant.
1 want / in / Do / holidays / to / you / meet / the / ?
______
2 for / Why / days / we / don't / go / a few / camping / ?
______
3 what / know / Let / you / me / think / .
______
4 Tania / Hi / ,
______
5 climbing / I'd / go / again / to / like / .
______
6 my / can / tent / take / We / brother's / .
______

3 Separate the text into words and sentences. Then rewrite the email with the correct format and punctuation in your notebook.

> **Tip!** Always check your writing for spelling or punctuation.

heyjosedoyouwanttohangouttogetheronsaturdaywecangotothe newshoppingcentreshallicometoyourhouseatfourletmeknowsoonpepe

Hey Jose,

4 Correct the spelling of these words.

0 *swiming* swimming
1 shoping ______
2 wich ______
3 tenis ______
4 Wenesday ______
5 tomorow ______
6 bycicle ______
7 diferent ______
8 scool ______
9 begining ______

5 Put the words in the box in the correct place in the story.

> **Tip!** Use time words like *yesterday*, *after* or *then* to make the order of events clear. Use words like *but* and *so* to show how the events connect.

After   but   so   Then   ~~Yesterday~~

0 Yesterday Annie had a technology presentation at school, 1 ______ she got up late. 2 ______ she got to school, she saw her notes weren't in her bag. They were important, 3 ______ she phoned her dad and asked him to look for them. He found them in her room. 4 ______ he brought her notes to school. She was very happy.

EXAM TIPS: Listening skills

Listening Part 4: Three-option multiple choice

In this part of the test you listen to five short texts. You always hear the text twice. Each text is about something different, and the question usually explains who is speaking, who they are speaking to and what they are talking about.

Example:

You will hear ***two friends*** *talking about* ***their plans for the weekend.***

You then have to answer a question about each text, with three options, A, B and C.

Example:

You will hear two friends talking about their plans for the weekend. ***What do they both plan to do?***

A They are ***both going*** *to a* ***basketball match.***

B They are ***both visiting*** *their* ***grandparents.***

C They are ***both going shopping*** *with* ***friends.***

You can write your answers on the question paper. At the end of the test, you will have six minutes to put all your answers on a separate answer sheet.

Exam guide: Three-option multiple choice

- You have time before you listen to read the questions. Read them carefully because they tell you what you need to listen for.
- Underline the important words in the question. In the example the most important word in the question is **both**.

  Example:

  A They are both going to a basketball match.

  B They are both visiting their grandparents.

  C They are both going shopping with friends.
- When you listen the first time, try and decide what the correct answer is and circle A, B or C. If you're not sure, don't worry. The second time you listen you can check your first answer or decide for the first time.
- Sometimes the first time you listen you hear that one answer is definitely wrong. Cross it out. Then the second time you listen, just focus on the other two possible answers.
- Always give an answer, even if you don't know which one is correct. You don't lose points for a wrong answer.
- When you have heard one text twice, don't spend a lot of time thinking about it. Focus on the next listening text when it starts.

REMEMBER!

You will usually hear the people talk about all the possible answers in some way but this is a 'trap'. Only one answer is correct.

To avoid 'traps', listen carefully to every word. You will hear negative verbs (for example: *I'm not visiting my grandparents this weekend*) or things which are similar but not the same as the correct answer (for example: *I'm going shopping with my sister on Saturday*).

Listening Part 4 practice: Three-option multiple choice

1 Listen to the sentences. Write *Y* (yes) if they are positive or *N* (no) if they are negative.
E.01

1 ____ 2 ____ 3 ____ 4 ____ 5 ____ 6 ____

2 Is the meaning of the sentences you hear the same as sentences 1–6? Write *Y* (yes) or *N* (no).
E.02

1 I decided not to buy the shirt because I didn't like the colour. ____
2 It takes Martin a quarter of an hour to walk home. ____
3 It was sunny yesterday. ____
4 Martin is flying to Spain on holiday. ____
5 Paula's sister has got dark hair. ____
6 The teacher tells Eric to do his homework again. ____

3 Read sentences 1–6. Then listen and correct the information that is different.
E.03

1 Alex went to Scotland by coach last year. ________
2 Laia is going to stay in a hotel with her grandparents. ________
3 Donna usually goes to the bowling alley at the weekend. ________
4 Harry lost his bus pass yesterday. ________
5 Last week Megan saw a programme about bears on TV. ________
6 Tom has got a basketball match on Saturday morning. ________

4 Listen and choose the correct option, A or B. You will hear each text twice.
E.04

1 The teacher has got a problem with Sarah's homework because
   A she made a lot of mistakes.
   B she did the wrong page.
2 What's the weather like today?
   A It's cold and wet.
   B It's cloudy and warm.
3 What did Corrin and Vanessa do today?
   A They went out for a meal.
   B They went out with school friends.
4 How did Nico get home after the concert?
   A He caught the last bus.
   B His friend's dad gave him a lift.
5 What did Ollie buy at the shopping centre?
   A a new sports bag
   B some new joggers
6 What does Chloe's mother want her to do?
   A go shopping
   B tidy her room

LANGUAGE REFERENCE

Subject pronouns

Singular	Plural
I	we
you	you
he / she / it	they

- We use a subject pronoun before a verb.
  She is Brazilian. (NOT ~~*Is Brazilian.*~~)
- The singular and plural form of ***you*** is the same.

Possessive adjectives

Singular	Plural
my	our
your	your
his / her / its	their

- We use possessive adjectives to show that something belongs to somebody. We always use possessive adjectives with a noun.
  Our house is big. *Their school is fun.*

Verb *be*

Affirmative	Negative
I'm Turkish.	I'm not Turkish.
You're Turkish	You aren't Turkish.
He's / She's / It's Turkish.	He / She / It isn't Turkish.
We're Turkish.	We aren't Turkish.
You're Turkish.	You aren't Turkish.
They're Turkish.	They aren't Turkish.

Question	Short answer	
	Affirmative	Negative
Am I Turkish?	Yes, I am.	No, I'm not.
Are you Turkish?	Yes, you are.	No, you aren't.
Is he / she / it Turkish?	Yes, he / she / it is.	No, he / she / it isn't.
Are we Turkish?	Yes, we are.	No we aren't.
Are you Turkish?	Yes, you are.	No, you aren't.
Are they Turkish?	Yes, they are.	No, they aren't.

- We use ***be*** to identify or describe something.
  They're red. *He's Spanish.* *It's good.*
- We usually use contractions in conversation.
  We're from Canada. *She's ten.*
- We change the word order in questions; we put ***be*** before the subject.
  Is David OK? *Are you from London?*
  (NOT ~~*You are from London*~~*?*)
- We usually reply with short answers.
  A: *Is it blue?* ***B:*** *Yes, it is.* ***A:*** *Is it red?* ***B:*** *No, it isn't.*

Question words

- We use ***what*** to ask for information.
  What is your favourite colour?
- We use ***where*** to ask about places.
  Where are you from?
- We use ***when*** to ask about time.
  When is your birthday?
- We use ***how old*** to ask about age.
  How old is your father?
- We use ***who*** to ask about people.
  Who is your best friend?

whose + possessive pronouns

	Singular	Plural
Whose book is this?	It's mine.	It's ours.
	It's yours.	It's yours.
	It's his / hers.	It's theirs.

- ***whose*** asks about possession or ownership.
- We often use possessive pronouns to answer ***whose*** questions. They help us to avoid repeating information.
  Whose pencil is this? It's mine. (NOT ~~*It's my pencil.*~~)
  We don't use ***its*** as a possessive pronoun.
  Whose book is this? (NOT ~~*It's its.*~~)
- We use ***this*** (singular) and ***these*** (plural) to talk about things that are near.
  This is my pencil. *These are my books.*
- We use ***that*** (singular) and ***those*** (plural) to talk about things that are not near.
  That is my schoolbag. *Those are my pens.*

Imperatives

Affirmative	Negative
Stand up!	Don't stand up!
Open the book!	Don't open the book!

- We use the imperative to give orders or instructions.
  Come here, please.
- We use ***don't*** to form the negative.
  Don't write in your textbook.

LANGUAGE PRACTICE

STARTER

Subject pronouns and possessive adjectives

1 Complete the sentences with the correct subject pronouns and possessive adjectives.

1 My best friend Maria is from Paris. ___She___'s French. ___Her___ house is very big!

2 My name's Pablo. ________'m from Ecuador. I'm in ________ classroom.

3 Berat and Ahmet are Turkish– ________'re from Istanbul. These are ________ books.

4 My English teacher is John. ________'s from London. ________ classes are fun!

5 Susie, ________'re my friend! Today is ________ birthday! Happy birthday!

Verb *be*

2 Circle the correct form of the verb *be*.

Hi, my name [1] (*is*) / *are* Alicia. My favourite colour [2] *is* / *are* blue. I [3] *are* / *am* 12 years old. My best friends [4] *is* / *are* Laura and Eva. They [5] *isn't* / *aren't* from Mexico like me, they come from China. We [6] *is* / *are* at school today.

3 Match questions 1–6 with answers a–f.

1 Are you hungry?	d	a Yes, we are.
2 Is your school big?	☐	b No, she isn't.
3 Is he in the room?	☐	c No, it isn't.
4 Is she from China?	☐	~~d Yes, I am!~~
5 Are we 12 years old?	☐	e No, they aren't.
6 Are they Canadian?	☐	f Yes, he is.

Question words

4 Complete the conversation with the words in the box.

How old When ~~Where~~ Who

A: Hi, Mateo. [1] ___Where___ are you from?
B: I'm from Argentina.
A: [2] ________ are you?
B: I'm 13.
A: [3] ________'s your birthday?
B: It's in February.
A: [4] ________'s your favourite singer?
B: Taylor Swift. She's great!

whose + possessive pronouns

5 Write the words in the correct order to make questions. Then complete the answers with the correct possessive pronouns.

1 book / is / Whose / this /?
___Whose book is this?___
It's my book. It's ___mine.___

2 is / this / Whose / dictionary / ?
____
It's your dictionary. It's ________

3 calculator / is / Whose / that / ?
____
It's his calculator. It's ________

4 these / pens / Whose / are / ?
____
They're her pens. They're ________

5 notebooks / those / are / Whose / ?
____
They're our notebooks. They're ________

6 desks / are / Whose / those / ?
____
They're their desks. They're ________

Imperatives

6 Write the affirmative or the negative.

1 Write on the paper.
___Don't write on the paper.___

2 ________________
Don't use your calculator.

3 Use your dictionary, please.
____

4 ________________
Don't listen to your teacher.

5 Close the door, please.
____

6 ________________
Don't do your homework.

LANGUAGE REFERENCE

have got: affirmative and negative

Affirmative		Negative	
I've got	two brothers.	I haven't got	three sisters.
You've got		You haven't got	
He's / She's / It's got		He / She / It hasn't got	
We've got		We haven't got	
You've got		You haven't got	
They've got		They haven't got	

- We use ***have got*** to talk about possession.
  I've got five cousins. *She's got 12 grandchildren.*
- We usually use contractions in conversation.
  He's got an aunt in Mexico City.
  They've got a photo of our grandfather.
- We use the full form of the verb ***have got*** to be more formal.
  He has got an aunt in Mexico City.
  They have got a photo of our grandfather.
- To make the negative, we put ***n't*** (not) after ***have*** and before ***got***.
  We haven't got a big house. *She hasn't got a sister.*

Possessive *'s*

Singular nouns	Plural nouns	Irregular plural nouns
Beth's computer	His parents' house	The women's football team
Carlos's bike	The students' books	The children's favourite toy

- We use **apostrophe + *s*** to indicate possession.
  This is Andrea's notebook.
- We put ***'s*** after a singular name or noun and ***s'*** after a plural name or noun.
  Carla's phone (NOT ~~*The phone of Carla*~~.)
  His grandparents' house (NOT ~~*The house of his grandparents*~~.)
- Some plural nouns are irregular. To show possession, we add ***'s***.
  men's, people's, children's
- When two people possess something, we use ***'s*** after the second noun.
  Juan and Ana's family.
  Mum and Dad's computer.

have got: questions

Question		Short answer: Affirmative	Short answer: Negative
Have	I got a blue book? you got a blue book?	Yes, I have. Yes, you have.	No, I haven't. No, you haven't.
Has	he / she / it got a blue book?	Yes, he / she / it has.	No, he / she / it hasn't.
Have	we got a blue book? you got a blue book? they got a blue book?	Yes, we have. Yes, you have. Yes, they have.	No, we haven't. No, you haven't. No, they haven't.

- We use ***have*** + **subject** + ***got*** + **object** in questions.
  Have you got a bike? Has your mum got a cousin?
- In spoken English, we reply to questions with short answers.
  A: *Have you got a brother?*
  B: *Yes, I have.* (NOT *Yes, I have ~~got~~.*) / *No, I haven't.* (NOT *No, I haven't ~~got~~.*)

How many ... have you got?

- We use ***how many*** + **object** + ***have*** + **subject** + ***got*** in questions to ask about the number of things.
  A: *How many cousins has he got?* **B:** *He's got 30.*
  A: *How many brothers and sisters have you got?* **B:** *I've got two sisters. I haven't got a brother.*

LANGUAGE PRACTICE

have got: affirmative and negative

1 Complete the sentences with the correct affirmative form of *have got*.

1 I *have got* a dictionary.
2 We ______ six red pens.
3 My aunt ______ three sisters.
4 Mum and Dad ______ a mobile home.
5 You ______ 12 cousins.
6 Our house ______ five bedrooms.

2 Write the sentences in the negative.

1 I've got two brothers.
I haven't got two brothers.
2 We've got a new teacher at school.
______
3 My grandma's got ten grandchildren.
______
4 My best friends have got green uniforms.
______
5 He's got a bike.
______
6 We've got a big house.
______

3 Look at the table and complete the text with the correct form of *have got*. Use contractions where possible.

	Juan	Rosa
sisters	1	2
brothers	0	1
cousins	2	2
bike	1	0
computer	0	0

Juan [1] *'s got* one sister, her name is Cecilia. He [2] ______ any brothers. He [3] ______ a blue bike. Rosa [4] ______ two sisters and one brother. She [5] ______ a bike. Juan and Rosa [6] ______ two cousins. They [7] ______ a computer.

Possessive *'s*

4 Write *s'* or *'s* in the correct places in the sentences.

1 My dad bike is grey and my uncle bike is black.
My dad's bike is grey and my uncle's bike is black.
2 Natalia favourite colour is green and her sister is blue.
______
3 His grandparent house is big but his parent house is small.
______
4 Myra family are from India and José family are from Spain.
______
5 Juan and Maria English book is red. Their mum book is yellow.
______

have got: questions

5 Write the words in the correct order to make questions. Then match them with answers (a–e).

1 got / I / Have / book / an / English / ?
Have I got an English book? ______ *d*
2 bike / a / Have / blue / got / you / ?
______ ______
3 pets / Alex / Has / two / got / ?
______ ______
4 Catalina / brother / got / a / Has / ?
______ ______
5 big / got / house / Have / they / a / ?
______ ______

a Yes, he has. He's got two cats.
b No, she hasn't. She's got a sister.
c Yes, they have.
~~d Yes, you have~~.
e No, I haven't. It's green.

How many … have you got?

6 Write questions with *How many* for the answers.

1 *How many cousins have you got?*
I've got three cousins.
2 ______
My mum's got two nephews.
3 ______
We've got 20 teachers at our school.
4 ______
My best friend's got two sisters.
5 ______
We've got four subjects on Friday at school.

Present simple: affirmative and negative

Affirmative	
I live	in Istanbul.
You live	
He / She / It lives	
We / You / They live	
Negative	
I don't live	in Istanbul.
You don't live	
He / She / It doesn't live	
We / You / They don't live	

- We use the present simple to talk about facts, habits and routines.
  I speak Chinese. *He goes to school.*
  They study English.
- We form the negative of the present simple with the **subject** + ***don't*** / ***doesn't*** + **infinitive**.
  They don't speak English.
- We use ***doesn't*** in the third person (*he* / *she* / *it*).
  He doesn't do his homework.

Spelling: third person

- The third person form (*he* / *she* / *it*) of the present simple ends in ***-s***.
  eat – he eats *read – she reads*
- With verbs ending in **consonant** + ***y***, we replace the ***y*** with ***-ies*** for the *he* / *she* / *it* forms.
  study – she studies
- The *he* / *she* / *it* form of verbs ending in ***-ss***, ***-sh***, ***-ch***, ***-x*** and ***-o*** is ***-es***.
  kiss – she kisses *relax – he relaxes*
  finish – he finishes *go – she goes*
  teach – she teaches
- Some verbs have got an irregular spelling in the third person.
  have – she has *be – he is*

Adverbs of frequency

always usually often sometimes never

100% ⟵⟶ 0%

- Adverbs of frequency say how often we do something. They go after the verb *be* but before all other verbs.
  She's always happy. *He sometimes checks his phone in the afternoons.*
  We usually do homework after school.
- With ***never***, we always use an affirmative verb.
  I never go out with my friends on Monday.
- In questions, adverbs of frequency always come after the subject.
  Do you always have English class on Wednesday?

Present simple: questions

Question		Short answer: Affirmative	Short answer: Negative
Do	I like oranges? you like oranges?	Yes, I do. Yes, you do.	No, I don't. No, you don't.
Does	he / she / it like oranges?	Yes, he / she / it does.	No, he / she / it doesn't.
Do	we like oranges? you like oranges? they like oranges?	Yes, we do. Yes, you do. Yes, they do.	No, we don't. No, you don't. No, they don't.

- We form present simple ***Yes/No*** questions with ***do/does*** + **subject** + **infinitive**.
  Do you brush your teeth in the morning? Does she go to bed at 9 pm?
- We use short answers with *do/does*. We don't repeat the main verb.
  A: *Do you often go to school by car?* ***B:*** *Yes, I do.*
  A: *Does he live in London?* ***B:*** *No, he doesn't.*

Wh- questions

Question word	*do/does*	Subject	Verb
Who	do	you	live (with)?
What time	does	the party	start?
Where	does	she	live?
What	does	his dad	do?
When	do	they	play?

- We form ***Wh-*** questions with a **question word** + ***do/does*** + **subject** + **verb**.
  What time do you go to bed? (NOT ~~*What time you go to bed*~~?)
  Where does he go to school?
- We also use the question ***How often ...?*** to ask about frequency.
  How often do you play video games?

LANGUAGE PRACTICE

UNIT 2

Present simple: affirmative and negative

1 Write the words in the correct order to make sentences.

1 I / every / day / wake / up / at / 7 pm
I wake up at 7 pm every day.

2 gets / up / has / a / Antonio / shower / when / he
____

3 have / homework / Marina / Mondays / doesn't / on
____

4 don't / brothers / My / at / 8.30 pm / to / bed / go
____

5 lunch / school / We / have / at
____

6 my / with / homework / helps / My / dad / me
____

2 Complete the text with the present simple form of the verbs in brackets.

On Saturday mornings, Nehir [1] gets up (get up) at 9 am. She [2] ____ (have) a shower and [3] ____ (brush) her teeth. Then she [4] ____ (get dressed) and [5] ____ (have) her favourite breakfast: toast and fruit juice. She [6] ____ (not see) her dad on Saturday mornings because he [7] ____ (go) to work.

At 10 am she [8] ____ (go) to see her best friends, Beren and Ela. They [9] ____ (not live) near Nehir. She [10] ____ (go) on the bus to see them. Nehir [11] ____ (stay) at their house for about two hours, then she [12] ____ (get) the bus to her grandma's house. She [13] ____ (visit) her grandma on Saturdays because she [14] ____ (not see) her during the week.

Adverbs of frequency

3 Circle the correct options.

1 I ... early in the morning.
(a) usually get up b get up usually

2 I ... sports at the weekend.
a do often b often do

3 I ... lunch with my sister at school.
a sometimes have b have sometimes

4 I ... my homework in the evening.
a do always b always do

5 I ... burgers for dinner.
a never eat b eat never

Present simple: questions

4 Complete the questions and answers. Use the verbs in brackets.

1 Do you play tennis at the weekend? (play)
No, I don't.

2 ____ your cousin ____ to your school? (go)
Yes, he ____! He's in my class.

3 ____ your parents ____ Spanish? (speak)
No, they ____.

4 ____ you often ____ your phone? (check)
Yes, I ____.

5 ____ your aunt ____ in England? (live)
No, she ____.

6 ____ your sister ____ her school uniform? (like)
Yes, she ____.

Wh- questions

5 Complete the questions with the words in the box.

How often	What	What time	~~When~~	Where	Who

1 When do you go to school?
2 ____ do your aunt and uncle live?
3 ____ does your dad do?
4 ____ do you walk to school with?
5 ____ do you have exams at school?
6 ____ does your mum get up?

6 Match the answers (a–f) with the questions in Exercise 5.

a My best friend. 4
b From Monday to Friday. ____
c In front of my house! ____
d Every month! ____
e He's an English teacher! ____
f At seven o'clock during the week and eight o'clock at the weekend. ____

LANGUAGE REFERENCE UNIT 3

can for ability and permission

Affirmative		Negative	
I	can play the piano.	I	can't play the piano.
You		You	
He / She / It		He / She / It	
We		We	
You		You	
They		They	

- We use ***can*** to express ability or permission.
  He can play the guitar. (ability)
  Dad says we can play video games tonight. (permission)
- ***Can*** is the same in all forms. The *he/she/it* form doesn't end in ***-s***.
  She can speak Portuguese.
- We always use the infinitive without ***to*** after ***can***.
  They can go to school.
  (NOT ~~*They can to go to school*~~.)

can: questions

Yes/No questions	Short answer	
	Affirmative	Negative
Can I go?	Yes, I can.	No, I can't.
Can you go?	Yes, you can.	No, you can't.
Can he / she / it go?	Yes, he / she / it can.	No, he / she / it can't.
Can we go?	Yes, we can.	No, we can't.
Can you go?	Yes, you can.	No, you can't.
Can they go?	Yes, they can.	No, they can't.

- We change the word order when we form questions. We don't use ***do/does***.
  Can you use your dictionary at school?
  (NOT ~~*Do you can use your dictionary at school*~~?)
- We use the adverbs ***very well***, ***well***, ***quite well***, ***not very well***, ***badly*** or ***not at all*** to describe how we are able to do things.
  A: *Can you play the guitar?* ***B:*** *Yes, but not very well.*

Verb forms: *(don't) like, don't mind, love, hate + -ing*

- We use the ***-ing*** form of the verb after ***like***, ***don't like***, ***don't mind***, ***love*** and ***hate***.
  She loves reading books. (NOT *She loves ~~read~~ books.*)
  I don't mind going to school. (NOT *I don't mind ~~go~~ to school.*)
- We can also use nouns after these verbs.
  They don't mind geography but they love history.

Object pronouns

Subject pronoun	I	you	he	she	it	we	you	they
Object pronoun	me	you	him	her	it	us	you	them

- We use object pronouns after some verbs and prepositions.
  She meets my sister and I after school every day. – She meets us after school every day.
  I usually have lunch with my friends. – I usually have lunch with them.
- For animals and things, we use ***it*** (singular) and ***them*** (plural).
  Don't feed the bird! – Don't feed it!
  Do you read books? – Do you read them?
- We can also put an object pronoun after ***like***, ***don't like***, ***don't mind***, ***love*** and ***hate***.
  This is my new book. Do you like it? (NOT ~~*Do you like*~~?)
  I don't like Mondays. I hate them.

LANGUAGE PRACTICE

can for ability and permission

1 Write sentences with *can*. Then write *A* (ability) or *P* (permission).

1 Artem / sing / very well
Artem can sing very well. ____ A
2 My dad / speak / French
______________________ ____
3 I / use / my dad's / computer / in the evening
______________________ ____
4 My brother / dance / well
______________________ ____
5 Harry / play / the guitar well
______________________ ____
6 You / use my / phone
______________________ ____

2 Change the sentences in Exercise 1 to the negative.

1 Artem can't sing very well.
2 ______________________
3 ______________________
4 ______________________
5 ______________________
6 ______________________

can: questions

3 Look at the table and write questions and answers about Alberto and Sara.

	Alberto	Sara
take good photos	✔	✘
paint well	✘	✔
dance salsa	✔	✘

1 Can Alberto take good photos? Yes, he can.
2 ______________ ______________
3 ______________ ______________
4 ______________ ______________
5 ______________ ______________
6 ______________ ______________

Verb forms: *(don't) like, don't mind, love, hate + -ing*

4 Complete the text with the words in brackets.

My sister [1] loves going (love / go) to school.
She [2] ______ (like / study). I'm different!
I [3] ______ (love / see) my friends at school.
I [4] ______ (not mind / learn) new things,
but I [5] ______ (not like / take) exams and
I [6] ______ (hate / get up) early every day!

Object pronouns

5 Match questions 1–5 with answers a–e. Then circle the correct object pronouns.

1 Do you like listening to your teacher? b
2 Does your brother talk a lot? ____
3 Do you love hanging out with your friends? ____
4 Can your friends help you and your sister? ____
5 Do you always go to judo classes? ____

a Yes, he does, but I don't listen to *it* / *him*.
b Yes, I love listening to *me* / *her*.
c Yes, and my cousin comes to classes with *him* / *me*.
d Yes, I do. I meet *them* / *it* every day.
e No, they can't help *us* / *you*.

6 Rewrite the sentences with the object pronouns in the box.

her	him	it	them	~~them~~	us

1 I like hanging out with my friends.
I like hanging out with them.
2 I can't find my pen.
____
3 I like my aunt.
____
4 They can't see you or me.
____
5 I love chatting online to my cousin, David!
____
6 I visit my grandparents on Sundays.
____

LANGUAGE REFERENCE

Countable and uncountable nouns

- Countable nouns can be counted individually. They have a singular and a plural form.
  one apple – two apples *one book – three books*
- Uncountable nouns can't be counted individually. They don't have a plural and are always singular.
  bread (NOT ~~*a bread*~~) *milk* (NOT ~~*a milk*~~) *homework* (NOT ~~*a homework*~~) *music* (NOT ~~*a music*~~)

a/an, some/any

	Singular countable	Plural countable	Uncountable
Affirmative	I've got an orange.	I've got some tomatoes.	I've got some chocolate.
Negative	I haven't got an orange.	I haven't got any tomatoes.	I haven't got any chocolate.
Question	Have you got an orange?	Have you got any tomatoes?	Have you got any chocolate?

- We use ***a*** with singular countable nouns.
  a banana *a cat* *a snack*
- We use ***an*** with singular countable nouns when the noun starts with a vowel sound.
  an orange *an uncle*
- We use ***some*** and ***any*** when we don't know a quantity or it's not important.
- We use ***some*** and ***any*** with plural countable nouns. ***Some*** is usually used in affirmative sentences and ***any*** in negative sentences and questions.
  We need some apples. *He hasn't got any tomatoes.* *Have we got any carrots?*
- We also use ***some*** and ***any*** with uncountable nouns. ***Some*** is usually used in affirmative sentences and ***any*** in negative sentences and questions.
  We need some juice. *Marta hasn't got any water.* *Have we got any rice?*

there is/isn't, there are/aren't

	Singular	Plural
Affirmative	There's a quiz today.	There are some eggs on the table.
Negative	There isn't a quiz today.	There aren't any eggs on the table.
Question	Is there a quiz today?	Are there any eggs on the table?
Short answer	Yes, there is. No, there isn't.	Yes, there are. No, there aren't.

- We use ***there is*** with singular countable and uncountable nouns.
  There is a school.
  There is some cheese. (NOT *There ~~are~~ some cheese.*)
- We use ***there are*** with plural countable nouns.
  There are some potatoes. *There are four pizzas.*
- In questions and negatives we usually use ***any*** with plural countable and uncountable nouns.
  Are there any bananas? *Is there any milk?*
  There aren't any burgers. *There isn't any bread.*
- In informal English we can use the contraction ***there's*** but we don't use a contraction for ***there are***.

much/many, a lot of

	Countable plural	Uncountable
Affirmative	There are a lot of eggs.	There's a lot of cheese.
Negative	There aren't many eggs.	There isn't much cheese.
Question	How many eggs are there?	How much cheese is there?

- We use ***much***, ***many*** and ***a lot of*** to express quantity.
- We use ***much*** in negative sentences with uncountable nouns.
  There isn't much water.
- We use ***many*** in negative sentences with countable nouns.
  There aren't many tomatoes.
- We use ***a lot of*** in affirmative sentences with plural countable and uncountable nouns to describe a big quantity of something.
  There are a lot of vegetables. *We've got a lot of rice.*
- We use ***how many*** with plural countable nouns and ***how much*** with uncountable nouns to ask about quantity.
  How many carrots are there? *How much juice have you got?*

LANGUAGE PRACTICE

UNIT 4

Countable and uncountable nouns

1 Circle the correct options.

1 I've got an *apple* / *oranges* in my school bag.
2 Alba's got some *potato* / *meat* for lunch.
3 I've got a *banana* / *bread*.
4 He hasn't got an *cheese* / *egg* for breakfast.
5 We haven't we got any *chocolate* / *carrot*.
6 They've got some *pear* / *milk*.

a/an, some/any

2 Complete the sentences with *a*, *an*, *some* or *any*.

1 We need _some_ milk and _some_ eggs.
2 I've got ________ apple and ________ cheese for lunch.
3 Have you got ________ oranges, Mum? I want to make ________ orange juice.
4 We can't make a cake! We haven't got ________ eggs!
5 I want to make a sandwich. I need ________ tomato and ________ egg.
6 Let's buy ________ fizzy drink and ________ fruit at the supermarket.

there is/isn't, there are/aren't

3 Complete the conversation with the correct form of *there is / there are*.

A: Let's make a salad!
B: [1] _Are there_ any tomatoes?
A: Yes [2] ____________, but [3] ____________ any onions.
B: OK, that's not a problem. [4] ____________ some cheese and [5] ____________ ten carrots.
A: I don't want ten carrots in my salad! Let's make spaghetti!
B: Sorry! [6] ____________ any pasta!

4 Write sentences about the food and drink in the box. Use the correct form of *there is/there are* and *some* or *any*.

apples ✔ bread ✘ pizzas ✔ eggs ✘ water ✔ banana ✘

1 _There are some apples._
2 ____________________
3 ____________________
4 ____________________
5 ____________________
6 ____________________

much/many, a lot of

5 Circle the correct options. Then match questions 1–5 with answers a–f.

1 How *much* / *many* fruit do you eat every day? [e]
2 How *much* / *many* people are there in your family? [ ]
3 Do you spend *much* / *many* time checking your phone? [ ]
4 How *many* / *much* sweets do you have every day? [ ]
5 How *much* / *many* water do you drink at home? [ ]
6 Are there *much* / *many* bottles of fizzy drinks in your fridge? [ ]

a There are seven: I've got a lot of brothers and sisters!
b About two litres a day – more if I play tennis.
c There aren't any. We only drink water and milk at home.
d No! I haven't got much time to look at it!
~~e I eat an apple every morning.~~
f I don't eat any! They're bad for my teeth!

LANGUAGE BANK

STARTER

Vocabulary

Months

January February March April May
June July August September
October November December

Colours

black blue green orange pink
red yellow white

Classroom objects

board calculator chair dictionary
door notebook pen pencil poster
ruler table window

Language in action

Subject pronouns
Possessive adjectives
Verb *be*
Question words
whose + possessive pronouns
Imperatives

Writing

Useful language

An informal letter

To start: Dear + Mr (*man*) or Mrs/Miss (*woman*) + person's surname
To end: All the best, Best wishes
To join two ideas in one sentence: and

UNIT 1

Vocabulary

Family members

aunt brother cousin dad daughter
grandad granddaughter grandma
grandson husband mum nephew
niece sister son uncle wife

Describing people

Eyes: brown, grey
Hairstyle: long, short, wavy
Hair colour: blonde, brown, grey, red
Height: tall, short
Other features: beard, glasses, freckles, moustache

Language in action

have got: affirmative, negative, questions and short answers
how many … ?
Possessive *'s*

Speaking

Everyday English

Are you alright?
Cool!
Got to go!
That's funny!
That's so not funny!

Useful language

Bye!
Hey, (Evan)
Hi, (Lily)
How are things?
OK/Fine, thanks. You?
See you later.

Writing

Useful language

An informal email

at the start: Hi, Hey, Hello
at the end: Email me soon, That's all for now, Write soon!
contractions: I'm, I've, He's, She's, We're, Here's, Who's

LANGUAGE BANK

UNIT 2

Vocabulary

Daily routines

brush your teeth check your phone
do your homework get dressed
go home go to bed go to school
get up have a shower have breakfast
pack your bag wake up

Leisure activities

chat online download songs go for a bike ride
go shopping hang out with friends
listen to music make videos
play an instrument play video games
read a book/magazine take photos watch TV

Language in action

Present simple: affirmative and negative
Adverbs of frequency

Speaking

Everyday English

Go ahead.
It depends.
No problem.
Sure.
That's easy!

Useful language

Is that OK?
I've got one more question.
I've got some questions to ask you.
Thank you very much for your time.
That's interesting.

Writing

Useful language

An article
apostrophe **'**
comma **,**
capital letter **A**, **B**, **C**
exclamation mark **!**
full stop **.**
question mark **?**

UNIT 3

Vocabulary

School subjects

art design and technology (DT) drama
English food technology geography history
information and communication technology (ICT)
maths music physical education (PE)
science Spanish

Places in a school

canteen classroom ICT room library
locker area main hall playing field
reception science lab sports hall
staffroom toilets

Language in action

can for ability and permission
Verb forms: (*don't*) *like*, *don't mind*, *love*, *hate* + *-ing*

Speaking

Everyday English

Don't be silly!
I'm stuck.
Not again!
Not great.
Oh, dear!

Useful language

Are you sure?
Can you do me a favour?
Can you help me, please?
Do you need a hand with …?

Writing

Useful language

A description

for example
like
such as

LANGUAGE BANK

UNIT 4

Vocabulary

Food and drink

apples bananas beans carrots cheese chicken chocolate eggs fish fizzy drink juice meat rice water

Adjectives to describe food

cold delicious disgusting fresh healthy hot nice salty sweet unhealthy

Language in action

Countable and uncountable nouns

a/an, some/any

there isn't/aren't

much, many, a lot of

Speaking

Everyday English

Enjoy!

Here you go.

No problem.

No worries!

Useful language

Can I have … ?

Can I help you?

How much is that?

I'd like a/an/some …

Is that everything?

That's … , please.

What kind?

What's in the … ?

Writing

Useful language

A description

We use *and* to add similar information.

We use *but* to contrast different information.

We use *or* when there is a choice (usually between two things).

UNIT 5

Vocabulary

Clothes

boots cap flip-flops hoodie jacket jeans joggers shirt shorts skirt T-shirt trainers

Accessories

belt bracelet earrings gloves necklace purse ring scarf sunglasses umbrella wallet watch

Language in action

Present continuous

Present simple and present continuous

Speaking

Everyday English

It's a bargain.

It's perfect.

No, honestly.

You're in luck!

Useful language

Can I help you?

Can I see the … one, please?

Have you got it in a different (size/colour/style)?

I'm looking for …

It comes in …

What about this one / these?

Writing

Useful language

A description of a photo

at the back

in the middle

on the left/right

next to (someone)

LANGUAGE BANK

UNIT 6

Vocabulary

Sports

athletics basketball (mountain/rock) climbing
gymnastics hockey rugby running
sailing swimming table tennis
volleyball windsurfing yoga

Sports verbs

bounce catch climb dive hit jump
kick lift pass run score throw

Language in action

Comparatives
Superlatives

Speaking

Everyday English

Got them!
Look!
That's crazy!
What are we waiting for?
Why not?

Useful language

How much are tickets?
Let's book them.
Let's go.
Shall we go?
They're (£45).
What's the (quickest/best/cheapest) way to get there?

Writing

Useful language

A profile of a sportsperson

We use *also* and *too* to give extra information.
We use *also* after the verb *be*.
We use *also* before other verbs.
We use *too* at the end of a sentence.

UNIT 7

Vocabulary

Animals

Birds:
duck eagle parrot
Mammals:
bear donkey giraffe hippo horse
lion monkey mouse whale
Reptiles:
crocodile snake

Adjectives

beautiful clever cute dangerous heavy
huge large lazy light long
noisy quiet safe short tiny wild

Language in action

was/were, there was/were
Past simple: regular and irregular verbs

Speaking

Everyday English

No way!
Really?
Wow!
You're joking!

Useful language

How was (the school trip)?
It was (really amazing).
What about (lions)?
What was (it) like?

Writing

Useful language

A biography

A few years ago
In 2007
On 10 October 2005
When she was two months old.
Today

LANGUAGE BANK

UNIT 8

Vocabulary

Places in town

aquarium bowling alley car park cinema hospital ice rink post office shopping centre skate park sports centre swimming pool

Personal possessions

bus pass camera concert ticket headphones IC card keys laptop money passport phone portable charger tablet

Grammar

Past simple: questions

Past simple: *Wh-* questions

Speaking

Everyday English

Calm down.

Don't panic!

Gross!

Let's drink.

Useful language

Did you have it when you (got to school)?

Did you put it (in your bag)?

What did you do with it after that?

When did you last (have/use/see) it?

Writing

Useful language

A blog post

I didn't hear my alarm **so** I got up late.

UNIT 9

Vocabulary

Outdoor life

use a compass light a fire read a map build a shelter catch a fish find food and water pick fruit cook over a campfire identify plants collect wood

Holidays

apartment bed & breakfast (B&B) camper van caravan chalet cottage hotel tent youth hostel

Grammar

Future with *will/won't*

Present continuous for future

be going to

Speaking

Everyday English

Easy!

Forget that.

I'm on it!

You're unbelievable!

Useful language

What about a (film night)?

What are we going to do?

Why don't we (have a picnic)?

I'm not sure about that.

I'd rather not do that.

Let's do that!

Writing

Useful language

An email

at home

in the morning

in August

on Monday

on 1 August

at the airport

IRREGULAR VERBS

Infinitive	Past simple
be	was / were
beat	beat
become	became
begin	began
break	broke
bring	brought
build	built
buy	bought
catch	caught
choose	chose
come	came
cost	cost
cut	cut
do	did
draw	drew
drink	drank
drive	drove
eat	ate
fall	fell
feel	felt
fight	fought
find	found
fly	flew
forget	forgot
get	got
give	gave
go	went
grow	grew
have	had
hear	heard
hide	hid
hit	hit
hold	held
keep	kept

Infinitive	Past simple
know	knew
leave	left
lose	lost
make	made
meet	met
pay	paid
put	put
read	read
ride	rode
ring	rang
run	ran
say	said
see	saw
sell	sold
send	sent
show	showed
shut	shut
sing	sang
sit	sat
sleep	slept
speak	spoke
spend	spent
stand	stood
swim	swam
take	took
teach	taught
tell	told
think	thought
throw	threw
understand	understood
wake	woke
wear	wore
win	won
write	wrote

Student's Book acknowledgements

The authors and publishers acknowledge the following sources of copyright material and are grateful for the permissions granted. While every effort has been made, it has not always been possible to identify the sources of all the material used, or to trace all copyright holders. If any omissions are brought to our notice, we will be happy to include the appropriate acknowledgements on reprinting & in the next update to the digital edition, as applicable.

Key: CLIL = Content and Language Integrated Learning, FF = Fast Finishers, SU = Starter Unit, U = Unit, VB = Vocabulary Bank.

Text

U1: Text about the brother Bibi and Bichu. Reproduced with kind permission; Text about Cortes Circus family. Copyright © The Wallenda Cortes Circus family. Reproduced with kind permission; **U3**: Text about Cuban Ballet school. Reproduced with kind permission.

Photography

The following photographs are sourced from Getty Images.

SU: lukbar/Stock/Getty Images Plus; bowdenimages/iStock/Getty Images Plus; Jose Luis Pelaez Inc/Blend Images; Panya/iStock/Getty; Images Plus; lattesmile/iStock/Getty Images Plus; Renaud Philippe/EyeEm; LysenkoAlexander/iStock/Getty Images Plus; Adrian Weinbrecht/Cultura; Dmytro Synelnychenko/iStock/Getty Images Plus; **U1**: Peter Beavis/Stone; Stephanie Hager - HagerPhoto/Photodisc; Voisine/iStock/Getty Images Plus; Jon Anderson/Moment Open; bobbieo/iStock/Getty Images Plus; Echo/Juice Images; Image Source; Jutta Klee/Canopy; Compassionate Eye Foundation/Photodisc; Kemter/E+; STOCK4B-RF; -Panya/iStock; lolaira/E+; Vladimir Sagadeev/iStock/Getty Images Plus; Bernd Vogel/Corbis; shank_ali/E+; EMMANUEL DUNAND/AFP; Eamonn McCormack/WireImage; Pascal Le Segretain/Getty Images; Kevin Mazur/WireImage for MTV; Ben Pruchnie/WireImage; Sean Justice/The Image Bank; Bruce Laurance/The Image Bank; View Pictures/UIG via Getty Images; Westend61; Jinxy Productions/Blend Images; FRED TANNEAU/AFP/Getty Images; Kiko Jimenez/EyeEm; Bruno Vigneron/Getty Images; FRED TANNEAU/AFP/Getty Images; Patrick Durand/Sygma via Getty Images; mocoo/iStock/Getty Images Plus; Sean Locke/EyeEm; SEBASTIAN KAULITZKI/Science Photo Library; Big_Ryan/DigitalVision Vectors; **U2**: Prasit photo/Moment; Vstock LLC/Vstock; Picavet/Photodisc; wrangel/iStock/Getty Images Plus; Dragos Cosmin photos/Moment Open; Fabian Krause/EyeEm; Timothy Allen/Photolibrary; Gordon Esler/Photographer's Choice; monkeybusinessimages/iStock/Getty Images Plus; kali9/E+; Tetra Images; Hill Street Studios/Digital Images; 7romawka7/iStock/Getty Images Plus; mocoo/iStock/Getty Images Plus; ConceptCafe/iStock/Getty Images Plus; **U3**: Pascal Manoukian/Sygma/Sygma via Getty Images; AWelshLad/E+; Westend61; Eric Lafforgue/Art In All Of Us/Corbis via Getty Images; Education Images/UIG via Getty Images; Digital Vision/Photodisc; Paolo Negri/Photographer's Choice; Homiel/iStock/Getty Images Plus; Peerapat Tandavanitj/Moment; Absodels; Natalia Kuprova/iStock/Getty Images Plus; Nikiteev_Konstantin/iStock/Getty Images Plus; mocoo/iStock/Getty Images Plus; **U4**: Leemage/Corbis via Getty Images; CreativeBrainStorming/iStock/Getty Images Plus; EasyBuy4u/E+; Richard Coombs/EyeEm; ahavelaar/iStock/Getty Images Plus; rosabernardes/RooM; cookelma/iStock/Getty Images Plus; nathan4847/iStock/Getty Images Plus; Juanmonino/E+; Ekaterina_Marory/iStock/Getty Images Plus; LUNAMARINA/iStock/Getty Images Plus; Jill Clardy/Moment Open; Lisovskaya/iStock/Getty Images Plus; romrodinka/iStock/Getty Images Plus; efired/iStock/Getty Images Plus; Holden Worrell/EyeEm; Tom Cockrem/Lonely Planet Images; Jamie Stamey/iStock/Getty Images Plus; Blaine Harrington III/Corbis Documentary; Edwin Remsburg/VW Pics via Getty Images; Russell Monk/The Image Bank; Jon Lovette/Photographer's Choice RF; fcafotodigital/E+; KatarzynaBialasiewicz/iStock/Getty Images Plus; mevans/iStock/Getty Images Plus; Karly Pope/Moment Open; Marco Livolsi/EyeEm; Ragnar Schmuck; structuresxx/iStock/Getty Images Plus; MediaProduction/iStock/Getty Images Plus; 4nadia/iStock/Getty Images Plus; margouillatphotos/iStock/Getty Images Plus; Karlevana/iStock/Getty Images Plus; phloxii/iStock/Getty Images Plus; ivo_13/iStock/Getty Images Plus; ValentynVolkov/iStock/Getty Images Plus; valentinrussanov/E+; Rengim Mutevellioglu/Moment; jantroyka/iStock/Getty Images Plus; pedphoto36pm/iStock/Getty Images Plus; Penny Tweedie/The Image Bank; Naoki Kimeda/EyeEm; **FF1**: Vladimir Godnik; Vera Anderson/WireImage; **FF2**: bubaone/DigitalVision Vectors; Gareth Morgans/StockFood Creative; kenex/DigitalVision Vectors; Dorling Kindersley/Dorling Kindersley; lushik/DigitalVision Vectors; Hero Images; Barry Austin/DigitalVision; Gang Zhou/E+; Compassionate Eye Foundation/Chris Ryan/Tax; **FF3**: Michael Moeller/EyeEm; intraprese/iStock/Getty Images Plus; April30/E+; Davizro/iStock/Getty Images Plus; Wavebreakmedia/iStock/Getty Images Plus; Lisay/iStock/Getty Images Plus; Viktorcvetkovic/E+; Bill Reitzel/Stockbyte; Mike Kemp; AlekZotoff/iStock/Getty Images Plus; **FF4**: kelly bowden/Moment; Carol Yepes/Moment; Tim Grist Photography/Moment; Burcu Atalay Tankut/Moment; Creative Crop/DigitalVision; Creativ Studio Heinemann; Photographer Nick Measures/Moment; **VB SU**: Symphonie/The Image Bank; Chumphon Wanich/EyeEm; Erik Rank/The Image Bank; View Pictures/Universal Images Group; Nora Carol Photography/Moment; Dorling Kindersley/Dorling Kindersley; Peter Dazeley/Photographer's Choice; Tim Hall/Taxi; Steve Gorton and Alex Wilson/Dorling Kindersley; imaginima/E+; **VB1**: Jamie Garbutt/Taxi; PeopleImages/E+; Morsa Images/DigitalVision; Westend61; Moritz Otto/EyeEm; Andreas Kuehn/DigitalVision; Erik Snyde/Stone; Sam Diephuis; Patricia Hamila/EyeEm; XiXinXing/iStock/Getty Images Plus; Emma Early/EyeEm; **VB2**: Rasulovs/iStock/Getty Images Plus; Maskot/Maskot; Sean Justice/Corbis/VCG/Corbis; bymuratdeniz/E+; Nomad/E+; Maskot/Maskot; Jose Luis Pelaez Inc/DigitalVision; kali9/E+; sophie adams; cardiff; uk/Moment; Compassionate Eye Foundation/Rob Daly/OJO Images Ltd/DigitalVision; Tetra Images; Flashpop/DigitalVision; **VB3**: Tom Merton/DigitalVision; xavierarnau/E+; Caiaimage/Chris Ryan/OJO+; Justin Yoast/EyeEm; SilviaJansen/E+; fanjianhua/Moment; Hero Images/Hero Images; Caiaimage/Sam Edwards/Caiaimage; Stella; Erik Isakson; Ariel Skelley/Photodisc; **VB4**: Arisara Tongdonnoi/EyeEm; RedHelga/E+; Dorling Kindersley:Charlotte Tolhurst/Dorling Kindersley; IvonneW/iStock/Getty Images Plus; Paul Poplis/Photolibrary; Kuzmik_A/iStock/Getty Images Plus; Barry Wong/The Image Bank; koya79/iStock/Getty Images Plus; Science Photo Library; annick vanderschelden photography/Moment; Skarie20/iStock/Getty Images Plus; LAL/The Image Bank; John Borthwick/Lonely Planet Images; **CLIL2**: rolleiflextlr/iStock/Getty Images Plus; kitthanes/iStock/Getty Images Plus; Jupiterimages/PHOTOS.com>>/Getty Images Plus; porcorex/E+; stock_colors/iStock/Getty Images Plus; **CLIL4**: al_la/iStock/Getty Images Plus; Cosmin Rechitan/EyeEm.

The following photohrahs are sourced from other libraries/sources.

U1: Copyright © The Wallenda Cortes Circus family; Copyright © Gem Hall; **U1–U3**: Carboxylase/Shutterstock; **U3**: Copyright © Cuban Ballet school; **VB SU**: Copyright © Cambridge University Press; **CLIL4**: Carl warner/Fairbank Literary; **ICONS**: Prithvi/Noun Project; Agni/Noun Project; mikicon/Noun Project; Baboon designs, US/Noun Project; Tanguy Keryhuel, FR/Noun Project; Icons Bazaar/Noun Project; Adrien Coquet, FR/Noun Project; Vectors Market/Noun Project; TukTuk Design/Noun Project; iconsphere, ID/Noun Project; i cons, US/Noun Project; kim Eriksson/Noun Project; Lloyd Humphreys, DK/Noun Project; Delwar Hossain, BD/Noun Project; Kirby Wu, TW/Noun Project; Magicon, HU/Noun Project; Baboon designs, US/Noun Project.

Video Stills

The following stills are sourced from Getty Images.

U1: andresr/Vetta; Maskot; monkeybusinessimages/Creatas Video+/Getty Images Plus; **U2**: ImagesBazaar/Photolibrary Video; **U3**: Klaus Vedfelt/Image Bank Film; Ariel Skelley/Image Bank Film: Signature; **U4**: chizheffsky/Creatas Video+/Getty Images Plus.

Illustration

SU: Alex Herrerías; **U1**: Alex Herrerías; Chelen Écija; Antonio Cuesta Cornejo; **U2**: Alex Herrerías; Chelen Écija; Antonio Cuesta Cornejo; **U3**: Alex Herrerías; Chelen Écija; Antonio Cuesta Cornejo; **U4**: Alex Herrerías; Chelen Écija; Antonio Cuesta Cornejo; **CLIL2**: Antonio Cuesta Cornejo.

Cover design and illustrations: Collaborate Agency.

Video production by Lucentum Digital.

Audio production by Creative Listening.

Typeset by Blooberry Design.

Workbook acknowledgements

The authors and publishers acknowledge the following sources of copyright material and are grateful for the permissions granted. While every effort has been made, it has not always been possible to identify the sources of all the material used, or to trace all copyright holders. If any omissions are brought to our notice, we will be happy to include the appropriate acknowledgements on reprinting & in the next update to the digital edition, as applicable.

Key: SU = Starter Unit, U = Unit.

Photography

The following photographs are sourced from Getty Images.

SU: Radius Images; kali9/iStock/Getty Images Plus; Carol Yepes/Moment; Classen Rafael/EyeEm; s-cphoto/E+; RinoCdZ/iStock/Getty Images Plus; Classen Rafael/EyeEm; C Squared Studios/Photodisc; AigarsR/iStock/Getty Images Plus; **U1**: Westend61; abell7302/iStock/Getty Images Plus; m-imagephotography; Tempura/iStock/Getty Images Plus; Rafael Elias/Moment; SSC/Stone; Xose Casal Photography/Moment; Jose Luis Pelaez Inc/Blend Images; Gustavo Di Mario/The Image Bank; Anders Johansson/EyeEm; Floresco Productions/Cultura; Andrew Bret Wallis/The Image Bank; jane/iStock/Getty Images Plus; Kalle Singer; Juanmonino/iStock/Getty Images Plus; ImagesBazaar; Simon D. Warren/Corbis/VCG; Thomas Barwick/Taxi; Bruce Laurance/The Image Bank; Images Bazaar; aimintang/iStock/Getty Images Plus; **U2**: bamby-bhamby/iStock/Getty Images Plus; Klaus Vedfelt/DigitalVision; JGI/Jamie Grill/Blend Images; instamatic/iStock/Getty Images Plus; SolStock/iStock/Getty Images Plus; SolStock/E+; Jim Jordan Photography/The Image Bank; James Collins/Corbis; "Steve Debenport/E+; "Glenda Christina/Perspectives; FatCamera/E+; Lobro78/iStock/Getty Images Plus; Westend61; LeoPatrizi/E+; Robert Daly/Caiaimage; Morsa Images/DigitalVision; Jamie Grill/The Image Bank; JGI/Tom Grill/Blend Images; Juanmonino/iStock/Getty Images Plus; Nick David/Taxi/Getty Images Plus; **U3**: Jupiterimages/Stockbyte; YinYang/E+; Wavebreakmedia/iStock/Getty Images Plus; NikolayN/iStock/Getty Images Plus; uptonpark/iStock/Getty Images Plus; Klaus Vedfelt/Taxi; Jon Feingersh/Blend Images; Mint Images RF; Eri Morita/The Image Bank; Vanda9/iStock/Getty Images Plus; Compassionate Eye Foundation/London, United Kingdom; hartcreations/E+; Image Source; Dinodia Photo/Passage; Amos Morgan/Photodisc; alongoldsmith/RooM; **U4**: Dougal Waters/DigitalVision; letty17/iStock/Getty Images Plus; Theerawan Bangpran/iStock/Getty Images Plus; Derkien/iStock/Getty Images Plus; Magone/iStock/Getty Images Plus; rimglow/iStock/Getty Images Plus; Foodcollection RF; tc397/iStock/Getty Images Plus; MielPhotos2008/iStock/Getty Images Plus; vanillaechoes/iStock/Getty Images Plus; chengyuzheng/iStock/Getty Images Plus; ddukang/iStock/Getty Images Plus; Onegin/iStock/Getty Images Plus; Bartosz Luczak/iStock/Getty Images Plus; Astrakan Images/Cultura; imtmphoto/iStock/Getty Images Plus; Vladimir Godnik; Donald Iain Smith/Blend Images; Buena Vista Images/DigitalVision; Veronika Lipar/EyeEm; Axel Bueckert/EyeEm; Karly Pope/Moment Open; Arx0nt/iStock/Getty Images Plus; rez-art/iStock/Getty Images Plus; Teen00000/iStock/Getty Images Plus; Science Photo Library; IvanMikhaylov/iStock/Getty Images Plus; Simone_Capozzi/iStock/Getty Images Plus; joakimbkk/iStock/Getty Images Plus; Inmagineasia; Taiyou Nomachi/DigitalVision.

The following photograph is sourced from other library.

SU, U1, U3: Carboxylase/Shutterstock.

Illustration

SU, U3: Antonio Cuesta; **U1:** Alex Herrerias; **U1, U4**: Jose Rubio.

Cover design and illustrations: Collaborate Agency.

Audio production by Creative Listening.

Typeset by Blooberry Design.